CW01574652

MARTINA LAIRD

Martina Laird has worked extensively as an actor both on stage and screen. She has won awards for her work as Comfort Jones in the BBC medical drama *Casualty*. She was also nominated for her work on *Moon on a Rainbow Shawl* at the National Theatre. She has taught and directed on many acting courses.

Driftwood is her first play to receive a professional production.

Other Titles in this Series

Mike Bartlett
THE 47TH
ALBION
BULL
GAME
AN INTERVENTION
JUNIPER BLOOD
KING CHARLES III
MIKE BARTLETT PLAYS: TWO
MRS DELGADO
SCANDALTOWN
SNOWFLAKE
UNICORN
VASSA *after* Gorky
WILD

Jez Butterworth
THE FERRYMAN
THE HILLS OF CALIFORNIA
JERUSALEM
JEZ BUTTERWORTH PLAYS: ONE
JEZ BUTTERWORTH PLAYS: TWO
MOJO
THE NIGHT HERON
PARLOUR SONG
THE RIVER
THE WINTERLING

Caryl Churchill
BLUE HEART
CHURCHILL PLAYS: THREE
CHURCHILL PLAYS: FOUR
CHURCHILL PLAYS: FIVE
CHURCHILL: SHORTS
CLOUD NINE
DING DONG THE WICKED
A DREAM PLAY *after* Strindberg
DRUNK ENOUGH TO SAY I LOVE YOU?
ESCAPED ALONE
FAR AWAY
GLASS. KILL. BLUEBEARD'S FRIENDS. IMP.
HERE WE GO
HOTEL
ICECREAM
LIGHT SHINING IN BUCKINGHAMSHIRE
LOVE AND INFORMATION
MAD FOREST
A NUMBER
PIGS AND DOGS
SEVEN JEWISH CHILDREN
THE SKRIKER
THIS IS A CHAIR
THYESTES *after* Seneca
TRAPS
WHAT IF IF ONLY

Hannah Doran
THE MEAT KINGS! (INC.) OF BROOKLYN HEIGHTS

Branden Jacobs-Jenkins
APPROPRIATE
THE COMEUPPANCE
GLORIA
AN OCTOROON

Elizabeth Kuti
FISHKIN TROUSERS
THE SIX-DAYS WORLD
THE SUGAR WIFE

Rona Munro
THE ASTRONAUT'S CHAIR
BOLD GIRLS
CAPTAIN CORELLI'S MANDOLIN *after* Louis de Bernières
THE HOUSE OF BERNARDA ALBA *after* Lorca
THE INDIAN BOY
IRON
THE JAMES PLAYS
JAMES IV: QUEEN OF THE FIGHT
JAMES V: KATHERINE
THE LAST WITCH
LITTLE EAGLES
LONG TIME DEAD
THE MAIDEN STONE
MARY
MARY BARTON *after* Gaskell
MARY SHELLEY'S FRANKENSTEIN *after* Mary Shelley
PANDAS
SCUTTLERS
STRAWBERRIES IN JANUARY *from* de la Chenelière
YOUR TURN TO CLEAN THE STAIR & FUGUE

Lynn Nottage
CLYDE'S
CRUMBS FROM THE TABLE OF JOY
INTIMATE APPAREL
MLIMA'S TALE
RUINED
SWEAT

Winsome Pinnock
THE AUTHENTICATOR
LEAVE TAKING
PIG HEART BOY *after* Malorie Blackman
ROCKETS AND BLUE LIGHTS
TAKEN
TITUBA

Giles Terera
THE MEANING OF ZONG

debbie tucker green
BORN BAD
DEBBIE TUCKER GREEN PLAYS: ONE
DIRTY BUTTERFLY
EAR FOR EYE
HANG
NUT
A PROFOUNDLY AFFECTIONATE, PASSIONATE DEVOTION TO SOMEONE (– NOUN)
RANDOM
STONING MARY
TRADE & GENERATIONS
TRUTH AND RECONCILIATION

Martina Laird

DRIFTWOOD

NICK HERN BOOKS
London
www.nickhernbooks.co.uk

A Nick Hern Book

Driftwood first published in Great Britain as a paperback original in 2026 by Nick Hern Books Limited, The Glasshouse, 49a Goldhawk Road, London W12 8QP, in association with the Royal Shakespeare Company

Driftwood copyright © 2026 Martina Laird

Martina Laird has asserted her right to be identified as the author of this work

Cover image by Seamus Ryan; art direction by Louise Richardson

Designed and typeset by Nick Hern Books, London
Printed in Great Britain by Mimeo Ltd, Huntingdon, Cambridgeshire PE29 6XX

A CIP catalogue record for this book is available from the British Library

ISBN 978 1 83904 550 9

CAUTION All rights whatsoever in this play are strictly reserved. Requests to reproduce the text in whole or in part should be addressed to the publisher. This book may not be used, in whole or in part, for the development or training of artificial intelligence technologies or systems.

Amateur Performing Rights Applications for performance, including readings and excerpts, by amateurs in the English language should be addressed to the Performing Rights Department, Nick Hern Books, The Glasshouse, 49a Goldhawk Road, London W12 8QP, *tel* +44 (0)20 8749 4953, *email* rights@nickhernbooks.co.uk, except as follows:

Australia: ORiGiN Theatrical, *email* enquiries@originmusic.com.au, *web* www.origintheatrical.com.au

New Zealand: Play Bureau, 20 Rua Street, Mangapapa, Gisborne, 4010, *tel* +64 21 258 3998, *email* info@playbureau.com

Professional Performing Rights Applications for performance by professionals in any medium and in any language throughout the world should be addressed in the first instance to the Performing Rights Department, Nick Hern Books, The Glasshouse, 49a Goldhawk Road, London W12 8QP, *tel* +44 (0)20 8749 4953, *email* rights@nickhernbooks.co.uk

No performance of any kind may be given unless a licence has been obtained. Applications should be made before rehearsals begin. Publication of this play does not necessarily indicate its availability for performance.

Woodland CARBON
www.woodlandcarbon.co.uk
NICK HERN BOOKS
Printed on Carbon Captured paper

www.nickhernbooks.co.uk/environmental-policy

Nick Hern Books' authorised representative in the EU is
Easy Access System Europe – Mustamäe tee 50, 10621 Tallinn, Estonia
email gpsr.requests@easproject.com

ABOUT THE ROYAL SHAKESPEARE COMPANY

The Royal Shakespeare Company (RSC) is a leading global theatre company that sparks local, national and international conversations that build connections, create opportunities and bring joy.

We passionately believe that great storytelling can change the world, and that theatre offers its own unique form of storytelling: it's live and shared, and transforms a group of strangers into audiences who, together, experience a story come to life in front of their eyes.

We collaborate with the most exciting artists to tell the stories of our time, and through a range of programmes we nurture the talent of the future.

We perform on three stages in our home in Stratford-upon-Avon, in London and in communities and schools across the country and around the world.

Our transformative Creative Learning and Engagement programmes reach over half a million young people each year.

rsc.org.uk

@thersc
Registered charity no. 212481

New Work at the RSC is generously supported by Hawthornden Foundation and The Drue and H.J. Heinz II Charitable Trust

The RSC Acting Companies are generously supported by The Gatsby Charitable Foundation

Supported using public funding by ARTS COUNCIL ENGLAND

Driftwood was first performed at The Other Place in Stratford-upon-Avon on **17 April 2026**, produced by the Royal Shakespeare Company in association with Kiln Theatre. The cast was as follows:

CAST

SELDOM	**SHANE DAVID-JOSEPH**
TOM	**ZIGGY HEATH**
DIAMOND	**MARTINS IMHANGBE**
MANSION	**ROGER RINGROSE**
PEARL	**ELLEN THOMAS**
RUBY	**CAT WHITE**

All other parts played by members of the company.

MUSICIANS

BANJO, KEYBOARD AND SHAKER	**LEROY JOHNSON**
PIANO AND SAXOPHONE	**TODD BRAND**
ENGINEER	**HENRY HACKET**

CREATIVE TEAM

WRITER	**MARTINA LAIRD**
DIRECTOR	**JUSTIN AUDIBERT**
SET & COSTUME DESIGNER	**SADEYSA GREENAWAY-BAILEY**
LIGHTING DESIGNER	**SIMON SPENCER**
COMPOSER	**CHRISTELLA LITRAS**
SOUND DESIGNER	**TONY GAYLE**
MOVEMENT DIRECTOR	**KLOÉ DEAN**
FIGHT & INTIMACY DIRECTOR	**BETHAN CLARK**
DRAMATURG	**SEBASTIAN BORN**
CASTING DIRECTOR	**MATTHEW DEWSBURY CDG**
VOICE AND DIALECT	**AUNDREA FUDGE**
DRAMATHERAPIST	**WABRIYA KING**
ASSISTANT DIRECTOR	**SAPPHIRE JOY**
ASSOCIATE SET DESIGNER	**DELYTH EVANS**
ASSOCIATE COSTUME DESIGNER	**ZOË THOMAS-WEBB**
CASTING ASSISTANT	**CHARLIE METCALF**
PRODUCTION MANAGER	**KURT MOORES**
PROPS SUPERVISOR	**PENNY LANE**
COMPANY STAGE MANAGER	**ANNETTE WALDIE**
DEPUTY STAGE MANAGER	**KLARE ROGER**
ASSISTANT STAGE MANAGER	**FAITH TO**
PRODUCER	**JADE PARKIN**

THE ROYAL SHAKESPEARE COMPANY

PATRON

His Majesty King Charles III

OUR BOARD

Shriti Vadera
Chair

Andrew Miller MBE
Mark Thompson
Co-Deputy Chairs

Geoff Barton CBE

Sir Nicholas Hytner

Amanda Parker

Winsome Pinnock

Anna Sedgley

Professor Emma Smith

Jonathan Smith

Professor Ayanna Thompson

Nick Varney

Liz Vernon

The RSC was established in 1961. It is incorporated under Royal Charter and is a registered charity, number 212481.

March 2026

Characters
(*in order of appearance*)

RUBY, *thirties, Trinidadian 'mixed-race' or 'Red' as we say in T&T* (*light skinned*)
DIAMOND, *late-thirties – early-forties, Black/African Trinidadian* (*dark skinned*)
SELDOM, *policeman, Ruby's age, African or Indian descent Trinidadian*
PEARL, *late-sixties/seventies, Black/African Trinidadian* (*dark skinned*)
MANSION, *late-seventies/eighties, English expat, formerly attached to British Council or Embassy* (*white skinned*)
TOM, *thirties, American Navy* (*white skinned*)

Though shade is not often discussed in terms of casting – here it is actually more than mere optics. It is a major and continued legacy of colonialism (anywhere that this history has been lived) that resemblance to the colonial power affords some perception of privilege. Though resemblance can be interpreted in different ways, those sensitive to these cultures are able to read socially, culturally and politically into appearance. This play is located in that space.

Notes on the Text

Language: Trinidad Picong can sound like a battle, but it is a battle enjoyed by both participants. The challenge is to 'come good' and impress your opponent, if even at their own expense. The battles are carried out with a light, throwaway touch. Until they become serious!

(/) is to encourage freedom to overlap. But overlapping is encouraged anywhere appropriate.

Silences and changes of subject are also responses.

Notes on Pearl's Song

(Act Three, Scene Three)

The song is written phonetically as received via Christella Litras. The translations we found that yielded most meaning were in Hausa. A rough guide is below:

> Goodbye Mama, (Maliweh)
> Let go of me, Mama, (Bweniwe)
> Here's Salman
> Goodbye Mama (Maliwe)

This text went to press before the end of rehearsals and so may differ slightly from the play as performed.

ACT ONE

Scene One

MUSIC: Recording of the Stick Fighters' chant, accompanied by Kalinda drums.

Date: September 1956.

Downtown Port of Spain.

Front room of ALMA. Hybrid of styles, though more Port of Spain downtown 'rumshop' than Englishman's drinking club. A few armchairs and coffee tables are set out randomly with a bar set upstage.

Street entrance stage right and exit to the rest of the house upstage left. What windows there are have blinds down or shutters closed.

Before the lights come up, faint stage lighting subtly illuminates a large African looking wooden sculpture of a pregnant woman with ample breasts and butt, positioned on a plinth upstage centre.

Lights up, we discover RUBY. *She is dressed very smartly in her interpretation of the movie star looks of the day: to her mind a Trinidadian Rita Hayworth.*

RUBY *is looking with delight at a large ornate floor-standing radio. The vintage radio is obviously new to the space and stands out incongruously with the rest of the room. She laughs and touches it sensually. She bends over to switch it on. 'The Young Girls Today' by the calypsonian Sir Lancelot, comes on and she laughs again. She does a small dance with the radio to the music.*

RUBY *leans over to an electric fan positioned behind the radio and switches it on. She angles the fan so that it blows directly at her. She closes her eyes and lets the fan's air cool her.*

The radio continues to play.

RUBY *snaps out of this and bends to examine the radio again, finding the tuning dial. She goes through the stations, passing news of Eric Williams (the future first Chief Minister) and the People's National Movement's (PNM) first campaign in the national elections.*

RADIO ANNOUNCER.... The countdown to the 1956 general election is well under way, with everything to play for in the battle for governance of Trinidad and Tobago. Yesterday's rally at Woodford Square, saw the leader of the newly formed People's National Movement, Dr Eric Eustace Williams, greeted with loud cheers by his supporters. According to Williams, a victory for the PNM could propel the country towards self-government of our beautiful twin islands. However...

RUBY *turns the dial and bypasses other calypso channels finding a station playing jazzy American show tunes. She turns the music up high.*

Happy, she sings along to Rita Hayworth singing 'Put The Blame On Mame' from Gilda. *This develops into a little dance, as she gets more and more involved in her interpretation of Rita Hayworth's sexy routine from the film. Despite her choice of music her dance is still always flavoured with her own West Indian movements and rhythms.*

DIAMOND (*dressed in a smart cotton shirt*) *enters through the street door. He is laden down with crates and sweating. He carries the jacket to his suit over one arm.*

DIAMOND *stops short at the sight of* RUBY. RUBY *doesn't see him enter so he stands there taking full advantage of this, transfixed as he watches her dancing and enjoying the breeze from the fan.*

When the crates get too heavy, he kicks the door so that it bangs fully open and draws her attention.

RUBY *spins round, smiling excitedly towards the front door. She stops short when she sees* DIAMOND *and the smile disappears. He is clearly not whom she was expecting.*

They stand taking in each other from their opposite ends of the room. RUBY *bends to switch off the radio. She turns again to face* DIAMOND, *the fan still blowing at her.*

RUBY. Yes?... What you want?

DIAMOND. Alma.

RUBY. Well, yuh find it. Now what yuh want?

DIAMOND. You wukking here?

DIAMOND *smiles at her*

RUBY *doesn't deign to answer.* DIAMOND *shifts under the weight of the crates.*

Ah had better put dese somewhere.

RUBY. Who are you?

DIAMOND. I bring de delivery.

RUBY. The what?

DIAMOND. Dis. De delivery. Look, ah really need to put down dese bottles. Dis ting doh play it heavy.

RUBY. Delivery? Where's Mahadeo?

DIAMOND. Who?

RUBY. Mahadeo. Who de hell you is for true?

DIAMOND. Oh ho. Mahadeo. Yes well, I's be wukkin' for he today coz he had was to go off some next place. Me ain't know.

RUBY *looks at* DIAMOND *trying to suss him out.*

RUBY. Through there. Just rest them down in de back so.

Holding eye contact with her as he crosses the room.

DIAMOND. Oui papa. Look at dat. Now dat is radio fadder!

RUBY *does not respond.* DIAMOND *exits to the back.*

A noise at the front door spins her round again. She laughs when she sees SELDOM. SELDOM (*dressed in his police uniform*) *laughs back at her.*

SELDOM. If dat tourist ship doh leave soon, dat man look like he goin' and swim de whole way back to Englan' by he damn self!

SELDOM *and* RUBY *collapse in laughter.*

Oh lawd. Dat was de best one yet. God gyal, yuh bad too good!

RUBY *laughs and walks to pick up her handbag.*

RUBY. Who could ah thought dat man face could ah turn even more white!

SELDOM. Girl, all dem flim you does be watching, is like you could get a real Academy Award for de set ah acting you put down in dat place.

RUBY *squeals with delight.*

RUBY. I thought he was goin' and dead for true.

RUBY *sings again 'Put The Blame on Mame' as she rummages in her purse.*

DIAMOND *re-enters the room.*

SELDOM. Is not a policeman like me dat you need for business partner, is a doctor. Next ting you know is one of dese fellas go get a coronary heart attack on yuh tail.

DIAMOND *passes back through the room on his way for more crates unobserved by the other two who are in hysterics doing impressions of a heart attack.*

RUBY. Boy doh try and blame me. Is you waving dat blasted baton all over de damn place dat go give dem heart attack.

RUBY *has a wad off cash in her hand, which she tries to count out on top the radio. She has to switch off the fan then continues to count.*

SELDOM. Well, nothing go make dem limeys run like de sight ah a big black man/a crazy Indian wid he baton in he hand.

He makes sexual gestures with his baton.

RUBY. Ahm, in dis house I thank you to keep yuh baton where it belong.

SELDOM. How a fine craft like you go say dat to a man like me. I is a man yuh know.

RUBY *hands* SELDOM *a share of the money.* DIAMOND *crosses the room with more crates and sees the transaction. All three stop and observe each other.* RUBY *carries on but* SELDOM *keeps a sharp eye on* DIAMOND.

RUBY. You is man? Dat is de second mistake you make today.

SELDOM. Ahm, 'second'?

RUBY *laughs, moves to pour a drink.* SELDOM *counts the cash.*

(*Looking at money.*) But ay ay! Wait nuh. What goin on? You givin' seasonal discount or what?

RUBY *empties the bottle and hands him the glass.*

RUBY. Here. It's de end ah de bottle but de new delivery now reach.

SELDOM. Ahm. Excuse me? Where de rest? Doh tell me yuh spend it on dat big arse radio you get dere.

RUBY *puts the remaining money into her purse then turns back.*

RUBY. Seldom, doux-doux, dat little extra 'hand' I know yuh takin' from dese men must more than compensate for my slight deduction.

SELDOM. 'Hand'?

RUBY. Yes, hand. And de plan is that we share de hush money from dese tourists, ehn't(ain't)? So when exactly yuh was planning to tell me 'bout de extra yuh does make dem pay you once you's escort dem back on board de ship?

They confront each other in silence as DIAMOND *passes through for more crates. He observes the change in mood.*

Your choice, partner. Either we in business or we ain't. But believe me, it cost plenty to fuck me, and it go cost plenty more to fuck me over. Don't test me!

Beat.

SELDOM. Lawd gyal! You have de nastiest mouth I ever hear on a woman. (*He laughs.*) Oui papa. How dat nastiness go come out such a pretty mouth?

RUBY *continues to smile silently.*

A'right, a'right. But yuh cah kill a man for tryin' to look after heself. Times hard. And a honest, hardworking police like me have to fight all kind ah temptation. But a little taste of dat niceness yuh have is all I need to curb dis greed and satisfy dis longing.

RUBY. I done tell you already, doh feel you go be wavin' dat baton round in dis house.

SELDOM. Is not only Roosevelt who could 'speak soft and carry a big stick', y'know.

RUBY. Yes, but you's a loud mouth and de stick soft.

SELDOM. Aye yie yie. Doux-doux darlin', you know ah love ya and is so you does treat meh bad…

SELDOM *laughs.* RUBY *laughs and switches attention back on the fan.*

RUBY. Hear nuh. Yuh know Lorraine dat have dat light skin baby. How old de chile is?

SELDOM. I ain't know. Must be 'bout six months or so. Why? What?

RUBY. Yuh ain't remember de Canadian from like this time last year?

SELDOM. Yeah, yeah. De one wid dem tick tick glasses and de bosey back.

RUBY. Eh heh. Apparently he reachin' back here again. I know I leave dat one sweet-sweet for me still. Buh we can't make dis same play again. That ain't go work twice. I figure this time I go touch he for child maintenance. (*Enacts.*) 'Oh daddy, I'm so glad you come back and see Junior. Look, he have your eyes.'

SELDOM *puts his fingers round his eyes like glasses and enacts a near-sighted man trying to see the baby.*

'Yeah, look… real close.'

They laugh. DIAMOND *comes back in, more crates.* RUBY *watches him as he comes in. They hold eye contact. He exits to back of house.*

SELDOM (*laughs*). True, dat man eyesight so weak ah feel he go fall for dat one easy. Plus, you have de man so bazodee. Is like dat ting yuh have dere does leave dem possess.

RUBY. Is dey own damn fault if dey want tings dey know dey can't get. Yuh can't sucker a fool who doh want to be suckered.

SELDOM. Girl you cold. But is so me like yuh. (*He checks his watch.*) Hear nuh, I ain't goin' see Lorraine, you know. I had was to tell you, they sending me Rio Claro.

RUBY. Rio Claro?

SELDOM. Eh heh. War done long time but dem Yankees does still be getting on like dey own de place. And dey feel us 'locals' must be grateful to them cause dem building we road and ting. Don't mind is we own asphalt from de damn Pitch Lake they using to build de road, eh.

RUBY. So what dat have to do with you?

SELDOM. Well, last week somebody break into de office and take de payroll. Now de government have to send police reinforcements to watch de place. And I-self get posted all de way quite in Rio Claro, to act like bodyguard to dem damn Yankees.

RUBY. What? How long you goin' to be gone?

SELDOM. Dat is de ting girl, I doh know. How long it does take to build a road?

RUBY. But now is the time for us to get real busy. Tourism going mad. Big ships coming in all now. It have plenty money to make.

DIAMOND *enters hot and tired, carrying his jacket. The job is done. He looks at the other two deep in debate. He takes out a handkerchief and dries himself. Looks around at the house taking it all in. He turns the fan towards himself and sits down on one of the armchairs.*

SELDOM. Oh God girl, I know. It real killing me. But what I go do?

RUBY. Well, what about tonight?

SELDOM *shakes his head.*

What! Tonight is big tings for us, man. You not here tonight? / You serious?

SELDOM. Rubes, I gone. Soon as I done here. They sending my whole barrack out dere in a army bus. / What I go do?

RUBY. But tonight. Seldom / …

SELDOM. Ruby, I tell you it hurting me bad to leave yuh, girl. And I know we could ah real clean up in Port Ah Spain. Doh blame me, blame whoever damn arse, country hooligan it is go and rob de payroll. Look, wait for me to reach back and we go still hit it big.

RUBY. Wait? I don't have time to wait. Look at me, Seldom. (*Indicating her body.*) This is all I got and, true, is peak but it ain't goin' last forever. I been doing this too much years, my time is almost up. I don't have no time to wait, y'hear me.

SELDOM. And I don't have time to stay. Ruby girl, you know is most tings I would do for you but if I ain't go now I go loss meh job at best or get lock up at worst. And true ting, you ain't goin' wait for me to come out no prison.

They regard each other.

Watch meh, ah gone.

RUBY *stands frustrated as* SELDOM *leaves.*

Doh miss meh too much, yuh hear.

SELDOM *smiles. It is not returned by* RUBY. *He leaves singing 'Brown Skin Girl' by Harry Belafonte.*

RUBY *stands fixed towards the front door. She turns and is shocked to see* DIAMOND *sat in the armchair with the fan towards him, observing her. He has unbuttoned his shirt and holds it open to let the fan cool him down. She stops and looks at him.*

DIAMOND. Ruby, so, dat is yuh name? Ruby? Yes, I could see dat make sense.

RUBY. If you're quite finished, shouldn't you be going somewhere?

DIAMOND. Ahm, no. I don't think so.

RUBY. Excuse me?

DIAMOND. Me ain't have nowhere I really need to be right now. I figure I could just cool mehself here for a bit.

RUBY. What?

DIAMOND. I waitin' for Miss Pearl.

RUBY. Why?

DIAMOND. Ehn't is she what own dis house.

RUBY. Miss Pearl? (*she laughs*)

DIAMOND. Yeah. Is business I have wid she.

RUBY. Oh ho. I see. (*getting her bag*) How much?

DIAMOND. Nah nah nah. Me have business wid she alone. I go wait.

RUBY. What it is you want, for true?

DIAMOND. Dis place… real nice. Why dey call it 'Alma'?

RUBY. Listen boy, you don't worry yourself with this house. This is the kind of place you really can't afford to be.

DIAMOND. I could give my whole life to have a house like dis and die a happy man.

RUBY *laughs scornfully.*

Mahadeo tell me Miss Pearl does run some kind of a drinkin' club here, not so? Gimme a drink nah. You wukkin for she or what?

RUBY. I think you'll find you made a slight mistake. This place is for members. Not for the likes of you.

DIAMOND. What is de likes ah me exactly? Tell meh, nuh. Coz I see yuh watchin' meh hard. So I figure yuh must like de likes.

RUBY. Boy, you can't be serious.

DIAMOND. I know dat look. My whole life me have woman watchin' me so. Like how dem hungry pothound in de street does watch when yuh eat yuh doubles, with de curry sauce running down yuh hand so.

DIAMOND *slowly demonstrates, licking his arm.*

You see dem dog watch yuh hard…

RUBY. Okay, that make sense, so is a set of dog does come behind you.

DIAMOND. I go show yuh 'dog' for true, if you let me come behind you.

RUBY. Boy, you had just best leave right now.

DIAMOND. Meh cah leave, I tell yuh.

RUBY (*laughing*). Boy, you good yes.

DIAMOND. Is who you keep callin' 'boy' so?

RUBY. Well which one of us look like a boy to you? Is only two ah we here.

RUBY *laughs at him.*

DIAMOND. Well dahlin' dat is where yuh wrong. Coz when yuh see me here so, is man yuh lookin' at. Y'understand.

Dis here is plenty man. Watch me good. Dis is more man than you ever see.

RUBY. Boy, like you real smelling yuhself.

DIAMOND (*flips suddenly*). You ain't hear me or what. I tell yuh I ain't no fuckin' boy. I look like some blasted child to you. I is a big man. So doh feel you go talk to me any old how. Coz I go show you what man could do. So watch yuh mouth. Yuh hear me?

RUBY *observes him interestedly. She got to him and she wasn't even trying. She smiles. This could work.*

RUBY. What's your name?

DIAMOND (*watching her closely*). Diamond.

RUBY (*surprised*). Diamond? Where you get a name like that?

DIAMOND. Same place you get yours, nuh. From meh mother.

RUBY. Diamond. Yes. And are you?

DIAMOND. Eh?

RUBY (*scoffs*). Nothing. You want a drink?

DIAMOND *looks at her, unsure of the sudden change.*

Well you said you're waiting for Miss Pearl. The old batch of rum finish but you just brought a whole new load so we might as well bus' it open. What yuh say…Diamond?

DIAMOND. A'right.

RUBY. Nice. But you know she not goin' to be back till quite tonight.

DIAMOND. Doh you worry 'bout dat. I ain't goin' nowhere.

RUBY. Okay. That's good. But meanwhile, there's a little something I think you could help me out with. Man like you, is jus what I need. It's true.

DIAMOND. Eh heh? What ting that?

RUBY. I been left high and dry. As you might have overheard just now. But not to worry, we'll still be back in time for you to see Miss Pearl about your business.

DIAMOND *looks at her and smiles, still taken aback.*

And you know, this thing go work out good for you too. Really. It works both ways. Trust me. What yuh sayin', Diamond? You good?

DIAMOND *laughs.*

Alright, doux-doux. Let me get yuh drink. Den we go talk and I'll tell you the plan.

RUBY *exits to the back.* DIAMOND *sits in the chair with the fan still blowing on him and looks around the room. He flips on the radio. He laughs to himself as he leans back into the chair.*

Scene Two

Much later that night, around 12.30 am.

The radio plays the calypso 'Wars of Long Ago' by the Mighty Spoiler.

Lights up.

The room now has signs of disarray: several used glasses etc. Guests have been and left.

MANSION *ambles about inspecting the room. A corpulent English man. He's been in Trinidad for over 40 years but is still suffering with the heat, despite it being night. He trains the circulating fan on himself and collapses into an armchair.*

PEARL, *sixties/seveties, had a hard life, smart dress but is barefoot as she walks about the house. She moves slowly and carefully, as though trying to not shake something painful inside.*

PEARL *pours him a drink from one of the new bottles as the final chorus plays on the radio.*

PEARL. Turn dat damn ting down, nuh. I can't even hear mehself thinking.

MANSION. Do as you please, milady. I've had enough revelry for tonight. I'd rather listen to your sweet cooing, my tropical nightingale.

PEARL *bends over to reach the radio switch.*

(*Regarding her from behind.*) Ahhh. Behold God's glory manifest before ye, sinners. Why don't you move that magnificence over here, share God's grandeur with this mere mortal.

PEARL *steupses. She hands him the drink.*

PEARL. Man, catch yuhself. Dem days done. Long done.

She turns off the fan.

MANSION. Woman, what on Earth are you doing? Do you want me to swelter to death in this infernal furnace.

PEARL. I can't take dis ting blowin'-blowin' all de time, givin' me a fresh cold.

MANSION. Sufferance. No respite. The devil's raking over the coals. No bloody respite.

PEARL *moves about the room collecting glasses, removing antimacassars and tidying generally.*

(*Sips his drink.*) Christ on the cross. What blooming concoction is this?

MANSION *examines the contents of his glass.*

PEARL. De new delivery reach today. Is a good ting coz we done run out of the last batch.

MANSION. But what the devil do you call this?

PEARL. How you mean? I told you I had find a new supplier. Mahadeo bring de delivery today.

MANSION. Mahadeo? He didn't tell me about tampering with my stock.

PEARL. So what, he must tell you every damn thing? I told you I was changing supplier. What that have to do with Mahadeo?

MANSION. Ahh. Cool down woman. Hell is too hot already. Don't boil over.

PEARL. Well, doh get me damn vex wid yuh stupidness. Anyway, dis one is cheaper, so is savings I making. And is a independent fella who own it, so that good too.

MANSION. Well, if you feel that this stuff will actually sell…

PEARL. You have a problem wid how I running dis place?

MANSION. No…

PEARL. Since I running dis place tings good. And you getting yuh money from me every month, ehn't? I never miss a payment in all dese years. So…

MANSION. Appease yourself woman, appease, appease. A man's choice of poison is the key to his character. You don't spring changes like this on a man my age. You could kill a poor sod that way.

PEARL *tidies.*

So an empty house. Things wrapped up nice and early for you. Midweek I guess, eh?

MANSION *picks up a newspaper.*

PEARL. De Charlotte Street house go still be quite busy for a bit.

MANSION. Good. What have we taken there tonight?

PEARL. I ain't go for it yet.

MANSION (*continues reading*). No?... I passed by Alma twice on my evening rambles but failed to see you either time. You were gone so long, one supposed you were off doing the rounds

PEARL *doesn't answer. She continues clearing.*

(*Knowingly.*) How were things at the University tonight? (*no answer*) I suppose that's where you were. Watching Williams posturing and preaching his pipe dreams in the park? 'The University of Woodford Square', he calls it. Politics for the plebs. You must be one of its most faithful pupils. Eh, Pearl? Haa. What pretensions. (*No answer.*) He'll never do it, you know. He thinks he's heading for a landslide. This country is not ready for self-rule. With independence comes great responsibility. And there's your problem. The people. What one doesn't like to admit was that when slavery ended the slaves went nowhere. They just sat by the roadside and wept.

PEARL *checks the time. She walks slowly and silently to pick up an old pair of shoes. She observes* MANSION *as she sits to put on her shoes.*

PEARL. Mansion, you go be here when I reach back?

MANSION. Oy oy. Is that an invitation?

PEARL (*steupses*). I want to talk to you 'bout Alma.

MANSION. Ah? What about this house exactly?

PEARL. I know you thinking of relocating yuhself back in England.

MANSION. Ah, this. Yes, my dear. It's time to go home. Alas, I have too long neglected the familial land. I understand that things there need my attention. Even the war damage has not been properly addressed, I am told.

PEARL. But you been sending back money from here dis whole time. Where it going? Dat place must be some kind of palace.

MANSION. Haha. What's your concern, dear one?

PEARL. What happens here to us when you go back to yuh green and pleasant lands? You say you putting some damn estate rep to oversee. In charge of me. And money go still be going to you and de land in England.

MANSION. Never fear, my dear. You shall be looked after. This place will still be here.

The lights flicker. They both look up.

Hmm. I see you've time to find new rum suppliers but not to fix a light bulb.

PEARL. Jeez and ages, dat ain't no damn lightbulb. I telling you long time now, this whole place need rewiring. You's be sending all that money from here to yuh damn family or whoever and it ain't have budget to fix up this tired old wiring.

MANSION *does not respond.*

Mansion. Look, you have de house on Charlotte Street, next one on French Street, and now dat place in Mucurapo. And is me runnin' all ah dem for yuh, and dey running good. Bringing in a lot ah money. Not so? You is a rich man.

MANSION. What's your gist, old girl?

PEARL. You rich from all de money I make yuh. Me, and all ah de others. But dis place here, dis Alma, to my mind, I have a right to dis place.

MANSION. A right?

PEARL. From de time you bring me to Port Ah Spain, and I start work for you, dis place is my only home. While you was doing 'what the hell you want', is me what clean it up when it was all broke down, and den is my back breakin' to keep de business going. Meh whole life is working in dis place. My child born here. Is my blood stain dis floor. Is me what stay here in dis hard-road heat, me minding dis place from dem downtown badjohn while you enjoy de cool breeze up on Lady Chancellor Hill. You doh even care 'bout dis place again. You leavin'. You say you goin' 'home'. But dis is my home. De only home I have. My whole life. My history here. And de only future I go have is here.

MANSION. You Trinidadians and your flair for the dramatic. Oh, you are wonderful, my little Pearl. What a performance. That'd earn you a penny or two on the streets at Jouvay. But the one thing I cannot get you to understand, my dear, is there is no room for Old Mas' when you're running a business.

PEARL. We could negotiate. 'Cause I is a old woman now. I too tired to be running all over town, day and night, collecting money and running business for you and all dis bobol. You done get away wid doin' all kind a ting, to me, and to all dem others. 'Cause is me here in de dirt, doing yuh dirty work. I just asking you to give to me what I done pay for.

MANSION. What have you paid for, my little oyster? A right? What is Williams teaching you at that University? Is this all from that book of his? *Capitalism and Slavery* indeed. What a lot of tosh that was. That little old 'deafy' thinks he can be the voice of the people. The commission shut him up last year. And now he's running for government. Haha. It's the Butler Party all over again. At least they managed to lock that one up. This one will be no better.

PEARL. Williams is different. The PNM have their constitution all ready to go. You watch. You go be laughing out the next side of yuh face.

MANSION. Constitution. Haa. Is that what you have, my little oyster? Have you got a constitution for this building? You want me to cede all this over to you.

The lights flicker.

And you can't even keep the lights on. Fill me up before you go for the money from the Charlotte Street house.

PEARL *gets the glass from* MANSION.

But bring me back some of the old batch from there, will you. They must have some left. I can't palate this new brew of yours.

PEARL *walks painfully to the bar and pours another drink.* RUBY *enters through the street door. She is clearly in a rage but stops when she sees* PEARL *and* MANSION.

RUBY. Place empty so early? You back from collecting already?

PEARL *continues to pour the drink without speaking.*

RUBY *smiles at* MANSION. *She is making a good play at concealing her bad mood but overdoes it slightly.*

She kisses MANSION *on the cheek flirtatiously.* PEARL *looks on.*

I love it.

MANSION. Hello, Ruby Red.

RUBY. It's the best one I've ever seen. (*She kisses* MANSION *again.*) Thank you. Thank you. No more damn Rediffusion rentals. It's magnificent, Mansion.

PEARL *hobbles over with the drink.*

Good Christ woman! When you going to get a pair ah shoes to fit yuh damn yam-foot? Walking round de place like a barefoot monkey, what you expect? Yuh big foot cah fit back in de shoe again.

PEARL *hands* MANSION *the drink.*

PEARL. You go be here when I reach back? I want to talk some more.

MANSION. Then you best not be long, Mrs Williams.

PEARL *steupses then picks up her bag.*

PEARL (*to* RUBY). Make sure and sweep dis floor for me. It have tings for you to do.

PEARL *leaves.*

MANSION *looks at* RUBY *joyfully stroking the radio.*

MANSION. Is it the one you wanted, my Rubenesque Ruby?

RUBY. Oooh, it's better. It's even better. Thank you, Mansion. Do you want to hear something on it?

MANSION. You choose.

RUBY. Great. Leh we see.

MANSION *watches as* RUBY *bends over to switch on the radio, in much the same position that* PEARL *was in earlier.*

She turns the dial off the calypso channel back to her station. Fun jazz.

MANSION. Dance for me…

RUBY *dances to the bar and gets a bottle which she dances over to refill his glass.*

RUBY. What you think of the new supply?

MANSION *does not choose to answer this but happily drinks the 'new stuff' for her. The light bulb flickers and the power surge stops the radio.*

This house go fall apart some day, y'know. The way she have it. Mansion, doh leave Trinidad, nuh. Oh gosh man. If you gone that stupid old woman go run this place into the ground.

And I know she have she eye on taking this place for sheself. You know that? Eh heh. She plotting and planning.

I could run it for you, y'know, when you gone. And I ain't going to try to squeeze you out like she go do. I know what dis place needs: Me. Believe me. I'm what you need, Mansion.

MANSION. I'm sure you are, Ruby. Just what I need.

RUBY. Then why you letting that old fool run de things?

MANSION. Don't be so cruel about your mother. She does a good job.

RUBY. What? Oh Mansion! With her stupid bush rum and old hard back chairs. She not even born in Port of Spain. She doh know it like me. Port of Spain is changing, Mansion, trust me. Is not just these local koonoomoonoos no more. Is all kind of big-time foreigners coming in now. Rita Hayworth was just back here again making a next film. They see Robert Mitchum in de Calypso tents liming with that Beryl McBurnie. Princess Margaret last year. This place need someone stylish, who can give de people what they want. I would only have de good supplies: Johnny Walker scotch,

Harts whisky, Gordon's gin, French brandy. Man, we could be making cocktails like you does see in dem Hollywood movie. Fred Astaire and Ginger Rogers.

She does a little quick step à la Ginger Rogers.

MANSION. Oh dear no. None of that cocktail rubbish for me. So 'Yankee'. No, straight up, please. The beauty, my dear, is in the purity.

RUBY. Okay, Mansion. You tell me, how you like it. Then that's what I go do. And when you gone, you know I looking after tings how you want. Not like she. She want to have it all for sheself. You and me, both ah we out. Me in charge, you know you still getting nice little dividends every month. Wha' yuh think?

RUBY *playfully approaches* MANSION *holding his gaze.* MANSION *laughs and gets up slowly from the chair and readies to leave.*

MANSION. Ruby. You are an enticing illusion. And you think big. I like that.

But you, my gem, were made for dancing. Music and dancing. How could you dance for me if you were wearing out your pretty feet walking the streets of Port of Spain like your mother? You are a beautiful bauble. To brighten our lives. Music. And dancing.

RUBY. Where you going? Don't leave. Spend some time with me, nah. She ain't go be back for a while yet. I want to thank you for the radio.

MANSION. Ah, Divinity. It's the wanting to stay that means I must leave. Ah. If only.

DIAMOND *enters through the street door, exhilarated. Spots* MANSION *and stops.* MANSION *looks at* DIAMOND, *confused.* RUBY *turns away and pours herself a drink.*

Oi oi, who's this? Hmm. We seem to have a guest. But I have miles to go before I sleep. So, to all a good night. Send Pearl my regrets. I couldn't wait and I daren't stay.

DIAMOND *watches* MANSION *leave then spins round to* RUBY.

DIAMOND. So?

RUBY. So? So? So what? You fuckin' mad…

DIAMOND. Hold, hold. Just hold on. Wha' wrong wid you?

RUBY. Wrong wid me. You's a mad arse. Dat is wha' wrong wid me.

DIAMOND. What? We get de money, ehn't? So why yuh vex?

RUBY. Dat kinda shit go get everybody kill. You want to start boxing people you could just haul yuh arse outta here.

DIAMOND. Aw dat. Look, if I supposed to be playin' some angry husband, what you expect me to do? I come in and find some next man wid my woman, my wife? It have jail in dat. Somebody go have to dead.

RUBY. Get out.

DIAMOND. Listen, darling, I think yuh own game have you confuse. This is man to man business you dealin' wid here.

RUBY. What de hell you know 'bout any of that?

DIAMOND. Well as it goes, when it come to 'horn', I is a bit of a expert in de field. I just never play de husband before. Horner not hornee.

RUBY. Leave.

DIAMOND. But we have to sort out de money.

RUBY *grabs her bag and pulls out a wad of cash. She estimates half and thrusts it at* DIAMOND. *He looks at it and laughs.*

Nah, nah. Dat ain't what I mean.

DIAMOND *pulls another wad out of his back pocket.*

Dis need to count out and all.

RUBY. What is that?

DIAMOND. A little lagniappe. Something extra. Dat is wha' I get off him after you done run off screamin' and he beggin' me to not hit he again.

RUBY. What?

DIAMOND. I start yelling like a madman. And then, I don't know, but it was like I was goin' to bawl for true. I telling yuh, like I did actually feel dat shit for real. (*Reenacts.*) 'O Lord put a hand! Dat is my wife. I love that woman. I love she bad. Dat is my sun and moon. And now you go come and… You take she away.'

DIAMOND *fake cries and reenacts the pummelling for* RUBY. RUBY *is dumbstruck. Then she laughs.*

RUBY. You is a big fool. Who you feel you is, Humphrey Bogart? So how much he give yuh?

DIAMOND. Here, baby. Take de ting. I givin' it to you.

RUBY. What?

DIAMOND. Nice little bonus? A little backhand does get a bigger hand. What you feel? We does work good together or what?

RUBY. Could be. Yuh bring a certain something. But I can't take no violence.

DIAMOND. Don't 'fraid. It not real. I ehn't never go hurt you, Rubes.

RUBY. I hear that before.

DIAMOND. What? Somebody do you someting? Who do you what? (*She laughs.*) Dat cah happen with me around. Ruby, look at you. Dat is precious gems. If even is play we playing, some man try to take you, I go feel dat for real.

RUBY. Feel what?

DIAMOND. Feel, I don't know what. But I see you and I feel something. Watch me in meh eye. You feel something?

RUBY (*pause*). No violence. You hear me? It shows no class. No style.

DIAMOND. Class my arse. I from Mayaro, some man gone wid my wife I ain't have no time for class.

RUBY. Mayaro?

DIAMOND. Eh heh.

He walks right up to her.

So look de tings. I just reach here and bam… stakes raise. I up de ante. So, what yuh say? You go show meh yuh hand? You show me yours, I go show you mines.

He leans in close to RUBY *and she looks him in the eye.*

RUBY. You best be careful how high you raisin' dose stakes.

DIAMOND. Dahlin' dis done raise so high yuh could fly a Union Jack from dis pole.

RUBY *laughs.*

We go have to stand at attention and sing 'God Save de Queen'.

RUBY (*still laughing*). Nastiness.

DIAMOND. Okay. Then you show me how you like it, baby. You call de trumps.

They look at each other, weighing up the next move. DIAMOND *delicately touches her face. After an initial flinch of surprise, she leans her face against his hand. Suddenly, sounds of* PEARL *arriving.*

RUBY *breaks away. She walks to the bar and pours a drink, turning back to take in* DIAMOND *as she drinks it.* PEARL *comes through the street door clearly in pain.*

PEARL. Dis walking all over blasted Port of Spain goin' kill me. Mansion and all he damn houses all over de place go put me in my grave. I done. No more. So help me Lord, no more.

PEARL *carefully removes her shoes; the relief itself is painful. She spots* DIAMOND *as she rubs her feet.*

Who dis?

RUBY. He workin' for Mahadeo. He deliver de crates today.

PEARL. What? Where Mahadeo? He never tell me he have nobody workin' for him. He cah just be sending people in my house and he don't even tell me. Wha' de Hell.

DIAMOND *looks closely at* PEARL.

What he want? How he still here?

RUBY. He say he have business wid you. (*to* DIAMOND) So watch she, she reach. This is yuh Miss Pearl.

Beat. RUBY *goes behind the bar and starts polishing glasses etc.*

DIAMOND. You? Miss Pearl is you?

PEARL. Yes. I know you?

Beat.

DIAMOND. I is Diamond.

PEARL. Diamond?

DIAMOND. Yes. I is yuh son.

Silence.

RUBY. Who son?

PEARL. 'Is you?

DIAMOND. Yes is me. I come to look for yuh. I wanted to see yuh.

PEARL. Why?

DIAMOND. I feel if I see yuh face it go all start to make sense to me.

PEARL. What 'sense'?

DIAMOND. My whole life. It doh make sense. Living like if yuh have chain tie to yuh foot. I was wukkin' down in Guayaguayare, buildin' dem new big road de Yankees makin'. Hot sun beatin' down on meh head and hot tar burnin' meh foot. And it doh make no sense. We build de road all de way to Rio Claro and I turn round and watch behind me and see de heat raisin' off de pitch for miles back. And I turn back and I watch all de miles still in front. And I feel de whole of life madness on meh head. And as I stand lookin' at dat heat risin' in front of me, I feel like I could see meh mother in de shimmering. And she holdin' out she hand to me. And you call me 'son'. And say, 'come, I go bathe yuh head in cool water. I go wash dat dust from off yuh foot'. And as I watch behind me again, all dem boss man now look to me like dem is devil. And dat road only going to Hell. And I turn and watch me mudder and see she is a Angel. And when she tell me 'come', I just throw down dem heavy-heavy tool. And get me de Hell out ah dere. I come to see meh mudder face. Coz I know dat is when everything go make sense.

Silence.

PEARL. Well I ain't no angel.

Beat.

DIAMOND. Dis your house? Is a nice house.

PEARL. What it is you really want?

DIAMOND. If it have space, and you doh mind, I ain't go stop long.

PEARL. Stay here?

DIAMOND. I just want to see meh mother and den I go go, whenever yuh say.

No response.

Please, my head so confuse. I ain't got nowhere else. I can't go back to buildin' dat road, my soul go break.

PEARL. Stay here?

RUBY. You go turn away yuh own born son? Lord, old woman, lord!

PEARL (*this costs*). I don't want no trouble. Don't bring trouble in my house.

DIAMOND. I ain't got no trouble.

PEARL. And I doh have no money to give yuh. So doh ask meh for none.

DIAMOND. No.

PEARL. And you doh stay here for free. It have work to do.

DIAMOND. I go do anyting you tell me.

PEARL *looks him over coldly then leaves the room.*

DIAMOND *and* RUBY *are left looking at each other. Now what?*

ACT TWO

Scene One

24th September 1956.

PEARL *sits sewing, which she carries on doing throughout.*

She sings in French kwéyòl (creole)/patois as DIAMOND *enters.*

DIAMOND. Oui papa. Dat soundin' sweet.

PEARL *stops singing but doesn't look up.*

My nen-nen used to speak Patois. Is she teach yuh?

Nothing.

The light bulb flickers above.

Yuh see dat?

PEARL. What?

DIAMOND. How dem lights flickering so.

Nothing.

Is like it happening more frequently.

Nothing.

You want me try and fix it?

PEARL. You is electrician?

DIAMOND. No, but I's know a ting or two.

PEARL. It good jus' so.

DIAMOND. Alright. If it have something else need doin' though, I could always try and fix it up for yuh.

PEARL. How yuh mean?

DIAMOND. Well, you always tired, nuh. I just feel like you need a little help wid tings round here.

PEARL. Eh heh? Is what you want?

DIAMOND. How yuh mean?

He gets a broom and starts sweeping.

PEARL. Well, if is one ting I learn in dis life is when a person start telling me 'bout udder people or 'bout myself, I does listen hard 'cause is always demself dey really talkin' 'bout. Listen good and you go learn something dey doh want you to know. So, seem as you here telling me how much help I need, I want to know what 'help' it is you want.

DIAMOND. So, nobody cah help yuh do nothing?

PEARL. I quite accustom do things for mehself.

DIAMOND. Well, I here now. You doh have to be so again.

PEARL. You here now? Who is you? One ting I learn good, is only me to do for myself. Nobody does treat me like dem sorfy-sorfy lady. So, cause you reach, I now suppose to forget all what dis life teach me? I look stupid to you?

DIAMOND. Aright, aright. Forget dat. You is one hard woman, boy. Stubborn.

PEARL. Stubborn? Good. Is so me survive.

DIAMOND. Ha, me too. Stubborn so I stubborn. Dat's how me survive. I must be learn dat from you. Or else is just in meh blood coz is not like you was dere to teach me it.

PEARL. So dat is what you reach here for. Is guilt you want to guilt me? Survive? You want to stand there so, big and healthy, and tell me you survive? You damn lucky. You want to make me feel bad? Dat is why you come here?

DIAMOND. I wanted to see you.

PEARL. Well, you see me. Now what you want?

DIAMOND. I want to understand. I want a mudder.

PEARL. A what?

DIAMOND. How yuh mean? Everybody have a mudder. I just want a mudder.

PEARL. Well, I can't be that. What? You want me sing yuh to sleep? You want to suck at meh breast, you want me wipe yuh arse? Well, is too late for dat.

DIAMOND *is silent.* PEARL *rubs away a sudden cramp in her foot.*

DIAMOND. Is not good for yuh foot yuh know. Wearing dem tight shoes and ting. You see dem Chiney woman and dey, dey does bind up dey foot to try and make it small. And by de time dem woman grow big, de bone in dem foot does be all mash up and dem can't even walk.

PEARL. I look like a Chiney to you.

RUBY *enters and flips on the fan.*

RUBY. Dis heat have me deadin'. Place hot as Hell. Dat is why is only a set a devil you does find downtown. See me, I goin' join de heavenly hosts livin' in de cool breeze up on Lady Chancellor.

Old woman, is sew you sewin' dat dress again. How you so blasted cheap you cyah even buy yuhself a new dress? Doh tink I doh know is a set ah money you have hide here in dis house, eh. You can't take it with yuh you know. 'Shroud doh have pocket.'

PEARL. Shut yuh mouth. You too damn rude. Old woman my arse. Is you what go put me in my grave. You and all yuh nastiness.

RUBY. Nastiness? Dat is a good one. 'Mango doh fall far from de tree', y'know.

PEARL. If dat is de force-ripe fruit I bear, dey should ah chop down dis tree long time.

RUBY *laughs.*

DIAMOND (*looking at the sculpture*). What is dis ting you have here?

PEARL *doesn't answer.*

RUBY. What happen? You loss yuh tongue? Dat is yuh favourite story. Yuh want me tell him or what?

Beat.

PEARL. When I was a chile in Mayaro, it had a old man call August what used to live next to meh aunt who raise me. He used to sit in de evening watching de sea and making tings from driftwood dat he find on de beach. Anyway, my aunt used to give me real licks. Bad. Real bad. One time when she beat meh, August find me hiding in he backyard, crying. I tell he how I wish meh mudder would come and save meh from meh aunt but me ain't have no mudder to look after me. August find dis piece ah wood one day, he say it must be float straight over from Africa, coz how it ain't have nothing else in de sea between Africa and Trinidad. He take de piece ah wood and he carve dis woman for me. He say is just so dey does make dem in Africa and he tell me dis here is meh mudder, straight from de mudderland and anytime I 'fraid, she go protect me and I must always carry she in any house I living in.

PEARL *starts to put on her shoes.*

RUBY. Yuh gone again? Where you goin' in dis hot sun? Even de wind blowin' hot.

PEARL *doesn't answer.*

Haha. Old woman, you good yes. Yuh goin' and vote, not so?

PEARL *bears the pain as she puts on her shoes.*

Well watch dis ting. Dis old woman goin' and vote for the first time. Next ting yuh know she turn politician. You feel it go make a damn bit of difference? What Williams could do? De man deaf and blind, and is him yuh want to lead de country? Allyuh people like a set ah pappyshow.

DIAMOND. When yuh reachin' back, Pearl? I want to bring a guy to meet yuh.

PEARL. Guy?

DIAMOND. Yeah. Dis American sailor I meet down Mucurapo when I went to de house for yuh. He was just wanderin' round like dem goat in de cemetery dat buss loose from their chain. I take he let we fire two rum in St James. And he tell me he looking for a central location where he and he navy buddies could hang out and so. I tell he come over here and check out Alma.

PEARL. You want to bring a set of Yankee in dis house?

DIAMOND. Dem Yankees here to stay. Is how much years de war done and dey still here. I tell you, if you dig dat well you go have water for days.

PEARL. Not in this house. Soon as you let in dem Americans dey doh leave. They does come on horseback but leave on foot. I ain't doin' no business wid them.

RUBY *mockingly sings 'Rule Brittania'.*

DIAMOND. Well, yuh crazy. Watch how de British and dem Americans workin' they thing. Right here in Trinidad. What you feel goin' on in Chagaramas? Is a whole piece ah Trinidad dey give dem Yankees to keep as navy base. But war done. So, what you feel really goin' on? If you smart you go fix up now.

PEARL. I ain't havin' no damn Yankee invasion in dis house, you hear me?

RUBY *sings from 'Jean and Dinah' over* PEARL*'s speaking.*

I done tell yuh already, we do things my way in dis house. Who doh like it could get de hell outta here. As it stay, I doh know why you still here. But you test me and I ain't care how much you cry 'bout mudder this and survival that. And how much guilt you throwin' at me.

I ain't 'fraid to put your arse on de street.

PEARL *picks up her things and leaves. Beat.*

RUBY. Well, that was touching. A mother and her son connecting. Maternal instinct real strong in dat one, yuh doh find?

RUBY *gets her purse and starts to count out the money into two piles.*

DIAMOND. You shouldn't cuss de woman so, yuh know. She is yuh mudder.

RUBY *steupses. She slaps one of the money piles into* DIAMOND*'s hand and puts the other back into her purse.*

Ay girl! Why so sour.

RUBY. I'm not sour.

DIAMOND. Wha' wrong? Yuh ain't find de ting work good last night. I ain't come in on time, or what?

RUBY. Oh no. No, actually you were nice and early. How come?

DIAMOND. Rubes listen. I find a next ting for we. Dis American sayin' if we fix he up it go have plenty business in it for we. We ain't go have to work dis small-time con game again. We set he up wid a little entertainment and we sorted.

RUBY. Entertainment? Oh yeah? So, who exactly on de programme? Me?

DIAMOND. Nah, none ah dat. Ruby girl, we could branch out. I have a feeling dis ting go be good for we.

RUBY. We?

DIAMOND. Eh heh. Wha' yuh feel, I ain't including you?

RUBY. Well, is you what meet dis Yankee and you ain't tell me nothing.

DIAMOND. But that is why I tell he come here so he go meet you.

RUBY. What he must meet me for?

DIAMOND. Wha' de…? Ehn't yuh just say how I ain't include you? Ruby, is you and me straight down de line, baby. Everything I do now is for de both ah we.

RUBY. I done have my own plans for dis place. What I need some Yankee for? Coming to tell me how to run tings in my own house.

DIAMOND. Ruby Red. Yankee and dem is real money. Girl, we thinking big. You want to eat a little tiny pie by yuhself, or yuh want a fat slice of a big backside pie.

DIAMOND *spins her round in a small dance.*

RUBY. You right about tinking small. I cah keep running these same games forever. And dis house is key. When de old woman gone, I could do real tings with dis place.

DIAMOND. Yes, and I here for all of it. I here for you.

RUBY. Hmm? Maybe. Well, I go make this place a real downtown destination.

DIAMOND. And I know you could do that. You got the appeal. But we deal with dis Yankee and get a little bit of US dollars on de side, we laughin'.

RUBY. But is why you change your mind about we strategy.

DIAMOND. I ain't change my mind, I just ready to try something different.

RUBY. Well, it look to me like you just can't be bothered again.

DIAMOND. How yuh mean? Ehn't I was dere for yuh las' night?

RUBY. You was there alright but you bounce in de place real early like you just want to get everything over and done. Hardly give me time to set up properly.

DIAMOND. How much time yuh want? If you ask me, I find like you movin' in real fast. Dat man was already stickin' on you like you is de Pitch Lake.

RUBY. But why you's be breakin' in de door earlier and earlier everytime? Is like you tryin' to make sure nothing ain't go happen.

DIAMOND. But dat is de whole damn plan.

RUBY. I know what de arsehole plan is. Is me what make de plan. You feel I want to always be compromising myself with them tourist man?

DIAMOND. Well then what?

RUBY (*breathes*). I find like dat ain't no set ah acting you doin' dere now. You comin' in vex for real.

DIAMOND. Well, me ain't want nobody touch yuh.

RUBY (*breathes*). Why?

DIAMOND. Why? Coz you ain't for dat. For dem sweaty tourist man to put dey nasty hand.

RUBY. Why?

DIAMOND. What 'why'? What I go say?

RUBY. I want you to tell me why you don't want nobody else to touch me. Tell me why.

DIAMOND. Why you feel?

RUBY *approaches* DIAMOND.

RUBY. I want to know.

DIAMOND. You is my sister.

Beat. They stand eye to eye.

I ain't lettin' no one…

RUBY. Why are you really here? Eh, Diamond?

DIAMOND. I come here to look for my mother. This is where I find she…

RUBY. You find she. And it ain't no set ah motherly love. So why yuh stay?

DIAMOND. I come here for she to call me son.

RUBY. Bullshit. She ain't want you here, why you stay?

DIAMOND. What?

RUBY *moves towards* DIAMOND.

RUBY (*breathes*). What else you want here?

She moves in closer and closer. DIAMOND *can't answer.*

A sense of family? A sense of belonging? What is it you want?

DIAMOND. No. I…

RUBY. I want you to tell me. You stay for me. Not she.

DIAMOND. I…I stayin'…

RUBY. You stayin' for me. I want you to stay for me.

DIAMOND. I stayin' for you.

RUBY. For me.

DIAMOND. Yes.

DIAMOND *takes hold of* RUBY*'s face and kisses her. She takes hold of him and they embrace.* RUBY *takes* DIAMOND*'s hand and puts it on her breast. He touches her and kisses her breast. It's almost maternal? They undress as they sink to the floor.*

The light bulbs flicker and hiss.

The light fades out as DIAMOND *and* RUBY *make love.*

Scene Two

The next day.

DIAMOND *and* RUBY *stand facing* TOM *who has just entered. He is tall and robust and shines in his American sergeant's uniform.*

TOM (*explores the room*). So, 'Diamond' right? This your place then. Yeah, yeah. I see what you're saying. I like it. This could work. It's got definite possibilities. What's it called again? Alma? That's nice. I think I had an aunt called Alma once, or maybe not.

DIAMOND. So, you find it alright then.

TOM. Oh yeah. No problem. It's a great location. Terrific.

DIAMOND. Yeah, dat is what I tell you. It could work, right?

TOM *backs into* PEARL*'s driftwood statue.*

TOM. Whoa. Well, hey now, who is this?

DIAMOND. That belong to Pearl, me mudder. Is art.

TOM (*observing the statue's ample parts*). Okay. Well… nice dimensions! (*Taking in* RUBY.) Hey there, how you doin'?

DIAMOND. Oh yeah, dis is Ruby.

TOM. Ruby? Great. Diamond and Ruby huh? This your girl?

DIAMOND. Uhm. Nah, nah. Nothing so.

RUBY *assesses this answer.*

TOM. Alright then. Hey. Call me Tom – (*Shakes her hand.*) So Ruby, you coming out with us, see the sights?

DIAMOND. I thought we could just fire one here first before we hit de road.

TOM. Great.

He collapses into one of the armchairs.

Yeah, I like this place. It'll do nicely.

DIAMOND. Ruby go pour you a drink. Wha' yuh say Rubes?

RUBY *contemplates this then moves slowly, silently to the bar.*

TOM. How much area is there out back?

DIAMOND. It have plenty man. And it have a yard too.

TOM. Uh huh. I went past the docks on the way here. Just so as I could get a sense of the distance. But hey, it's real close. Great.

DIAMOND. Dat is what I tell yuh, is real close to the docks.

TOM. You weren't wrong. There won't be any worry about getting supplies here off the boat.

DIAMOND. Yeah man. Uhm. What kinda supplies dat?

RUBY *approaches with the drinks.*

TOM. Why thank you, lovely lady. So, are you from round here too?

RUBY. Too? Yeah, I born and live here all my life. I born in this self-same house.

TOM. You don't say.

RUBY. Eh heh. Just 'bout right where you sittin'. My mother was trying to make it out de door but up to now she ain't reach and she had was to just drop me right there.

TOM. Wow. Great story. So, you are the bonafide article.

RUBY. I am.

TOM (*sips*). Jesus Christ. What the… What the hell is this stuff?

DIAMOND. Oh dat. Dat is some special local brew what Pearl, we mother, bring in from country. Fortified.

TOM. I'll say. Damn.

RUBY. I told her already, people don't want to be drinking dat bush rum nowadays.

TOM. Well, it's uh stimulating. It's got a kick. Hey. That's a swell radio you got there.

RUBY. You want some music, Tom?

TOM. Hell yeah, Ruby. Let's have some of that.

RUBY *switches on the radio. A calypso station comes on.* RUBY *plays with the dial and finds her American band.*

DIAMOND. Girl, is like you ain't like Calypso at all at all?

TOM. This is a good tune.

RUBY. Yeah, yeah. Kaiso good for Carnival time. But de rest ah de year I like to listen to real music.

RUBY *sways to the music.* TOM *observes.*

TOM. Goddamn. Now that's a beautiful thing.

RUBY *sees* DIAMOND*'s face twitch at this and enjoys it.*

So, Diamond, I got a real business proposition for you.

DIAMOND. Eh heh. Leh me hear it.

RUBY. You want me to turn off de music?

TOM. Oh no, honey. What I want is for you to keep doing exactly what you're doing. Don't you dare stop.

Seeing that DIAMOND *does not enjoy this,* RUBY *continues.*

Diamond, old buddy, I need to know if you're a man of discretion. A man with his own mind.

DIAMOND. Yeah man, for sure… How yuh mean?

TOM. I've got a proposal for you, buddy, that could make some people uneasy. Hey, there's no harm in it but I need an independent minded man who isn't afraid to bend the rules a little. A maverick.

DIAMOND. Yeah. That's me.

TOM. Hey, I thought so. Gunslinger. Okay. Here's the thing, Mr. D. This Alma place of yours is a spit from the docks. That kind of proximity, my friend, makes it valuable for storage of, well, imported merchandise, while they await further transportation.

The commodities in question will all be contracted onwards already. But because of the, you know, delicate nature of these dealings, we may need to hold them here in transit. Break it up a bit. And we need to do it discreetly.

DIAMOND. Oh ho. I see. Yeah, I get yuh.

TOM. Listen, there are some big guys running all this. Serious hombres. You won't need to concern yourself with the business sides, that's all done. But your Alma is an ideal lay-over. You can make some big bucks out of this and just keep your nose clean.

DIAMOND. Big bucks huh?

TOM (*holds up his glass*). Hey beautiful, how's about another hit. That stuff's crazy but it's doing the trick.

RUBY *gets his glass and saunters over to the bar.*

(*Looking at her.*) Goddamn! Yeah, we'll make it worth your while, for use of your base. For your discretion. Hey, you get in good with these business guys, it's going to guarantee good things for you. Join us. Come sit.

RUBY *comes back and hands him the drink. He takes it but holds onto her hand at the same time. She is surprised but he keeps hold and looks up at her. She stays put and he pulls her down to sit on the arm of his chair.* DIAMOND *turns the radio off.*

(*Noticing* DIAMOND.) I mean sorry, if you got your own thing going on, we stepping on your toes or you don't want our business that's …

RUBY. Well, actually, we do have a pretty comfortable setup already, as it goes.

TOM. Oh, I see. You two some kind of partners?

RUBY. Yes, we are. And I got plans for us. For Alma.

TOM. Okay. I get you. Well, I'm not trying to get rid of you, beauty. I'm not the kind of guy to waste a good thing. You got room for a third partner?

RUBY. We doing just fine with two.

TOM. But baby, why go it alone? Even the Great Brittania needed the U.S. of A. as an ally. These are some big dealers I'm rolling with, baby. You look like the kind of lady likes the good life.

DIAMOND. Dis storage ting. Like it need a lot ah space or what?

TOM. Well, those are what we call details. But listen, son, if there's a problem there are a whole lot of other houses round here. I can go somewhere else. Once we get going with this there's no pulling out.

DIAMOND. Nah, nah, nah. No need for dat. I is yuh man.

RUBY. Course there is the problem that this house isn't actually yours, 'Mr D'.

TOM. How's that now?

DIAMOND. Doh mind dat, man, doh mind dat. Is a family ting. Is we mudder house.

TOM. Well, from what I've seen so far, it looks like I'm sure going to like this family.

RUBY. Ha. Is joke yuh joke? You really don't know nothing. You feel is she own this house?

DIAMOND *is taken aback.*

TOM. What you saying, little lady?

RUBY. That's why you all sweet-up under she? You feel she own house?

DIAMOND. Who house this supposed to be? She run everything.

RUBY. She ain't have money to own nothing. Yeah, she work like a dog but is Mansion own dis dog house, and all dem house so.

TOM. Diamond, my good man, when we deal we gotta deal straight. You tell me whom exactly I'm dealing with here. Mansion?

RUBY. Yeah, a big old English man. Got she slavin' and thinkin' she run tings. She so stupid, she kill sheself for him and get nothing.

TOM. Diamond, c'mon kid. You don't seem to know what's what? But you know this Mansion, do you?

DIAMOND. Yer man, of course I know Mansion.

TOM. Ruby?

RUBY. I know he real good. When Pearl gone is me go take over dis place.

TOM. Now, is that so?

TOM *puts his hand on* RUBY*'s leg.* RUBY *flinches.* DIAMOND *does nothing.*

DIAMOND. You see, man. We doing business, or what?

TOM. Haha. Business yes, but with whom, Diamond? With whom?

TOM *strokes* RUBY*'s leg.* RUBY *looks up at* DIAMOND *for him to stop this, but he looks away.*

DIAMOND. Well, if we all go be doing business together, I think dat call for a little celebration.

DIAMOND *prepares to leave.* RUBY *glares at him but he avoids her eye.*

RUBY. Seriously? You're leaving?

DIAMOND. Forget 'bout dat bush rum though, leh me go down de road and get we a little something special so we could raise a glass. Allyuh stay here till I reach back.

RUBY *is stunned. Is he really going to leave her here?*

RUBY. Seriously? You're leaving? We doing business.

TOM (*hands still on* RUBY). I'm liking this better and better.

RUBY. Diamond, don't go.

DIAMOND (*to* TOM). Allyuh stay here 'till I reach back. But it might take me a while.

TOM. We get to spend a little time alone, honey.

DIAMOND *meets* RUBY*'s eye. She scowls at him. He says nothing, looks away and exits to the street.* RUBY *and* TOM *are left alone together.* RUBY *continues to stare at the front door after* DIAMOND*'s exit.* TOM *finishes his drink.* RUBY *collects herself and makes a choice. She turns to* TOM *and smiles. She leans way in as she takes his glass, touching his hand as she does.*

RUBY. Let me get you another.

Interval.

ACT THREE

Four weeks later:

As the Interval lights dim we listen to 'Trinidad Is Changing' by Sir Lancelot.

Lights up.

Scene One

The music fades into 'Man Smart/Woman Smarter' by Harry Belafonte.

RUBY *stands looking in glee at a new record player placed on top of the radio.* MANSION *observes.*

RUBY *dances.* DIAMOND *stands behind looking on.*

TOM *and* MANSION *sit at a table.* TOM *shuffles a pack of cards as the music plays.*

RUBY. It's terrific. Thank you, Tom-Tom.

TOM. Haha. Well, she's a great little gadget, honey. American best. The calypso record is in your honour. This song reminds me of you.

RUBY. Haha. I love it.

RUBY *throws her arms round his neck and kisses him.*

DIAMOND (*sitting at the table*). Calypso? Who calypsonian is dat?

TOM. That my son, is the one and only Harry Belafonte.

DIAMOND. Harry Who?

TOM. Harry Belafonte. C'mon, you know him, buddy. He's a Hollywood star.

RUBY. Oh god I love Harry Belafonte. Carmen Jones! I'm Dorothy Dandridge!

TOM. You sure are, Ruby Jones.

RUBY *grabs the nine of spades from the pack and ominously sings 'Da Niiiine' à la Carmen Jones to* DIAMOND.

DIAMOND. Buh wha' de jail? How de arse Harry Belafonte go be a calypsonian. Dat is a old King Radio tune.

TOM. Hey man, Harry Belafonte is the King of Calypso.

DIAMOND. De what! How a American go be King ah Calypso? Dat come like Mighty Sparrow feelin' he is John Wayne.

DIAMOND *switches off the record player. The others laugh at him.*

TOM. Yeah, you're a funny guy. Right, so who's in? Mansion?

MANSION. Mmm. Yes, my American friend. But one round, I'm afraid. I must go.

DIAMOND. Nice. Everything to play for. Rubes, you playing or what?

MANSION. Come on, my lovely consort. I can't play without a partner.

RUBY. Okay. Yeah, I'm in.

RUBY *takes a chair opposite* MANSION.

DIAMOND. So is you and me, Tom meh man. Good? Right. Mansion, I need you to cut or tap de pack for meh.

MANSION. I'll allow the lady the honour.

DIAMOND. Nah, nah, nah. Is dealer's left suppose' to cut.

MANSION. Indulge me. Allow my charming colleague to act on my behalf. I'm sure we can all still follow the game despite this minor infraction.

TOM. Looks like we got our own approach to rules in this house. I like that.

DIAMOND. Dat is good man. Tings sweet. Rubes, go 'head.

RUBY (*with sarcasm*). You sure?

DIAMOND. Just tap de top card.

RUBY. But I want to cut de pack. W'happen?

MANSION. I believe it is the lady's prerogative to choose.

DIAMOND. Nice. Just cut it nah.

TOM. Great. Talk me through it again. There're one or two points I didn't quite catch.

DIAMOND. I got you. So right. All Fours. (*He shuffles and then deals.*) A real good Trini game. De trick is to find dem surreptitious ways to only let yuh partner know what in yuh hand so allyuh doh end up playin' against one and other.

TOM. We've got this game. Pretty much. We call it Bridge. But that's a game for nice old ladies.

DIAMOND. Well, that's probably a matter of how allyuh does play it. Nice, so heart is trumps. Right. Mansion, I need you to cut or tap de pack for meh. Check yuh cards Rubes. You want me to deal you more?

RUBY. Nah. I ain't begging.

DIAMOND. Sweet. De rest ah allyuh could check yuh hand now.

So, yuh does have signals you could use to communicate wid yuh partner. Like if yuh touch yuh heart so – (*He clutches his heart like a heart attack.*) dat go mean yuh have hearts or if yuh press yuh three finger together so, that is clubs. Cup yuh hand for spade and slash so for diamond. Y'understand?

TOM. Yeah. I'd forgotten those.

DIAMOND. Doh mind. Everything to play for and you playin' wid a master. Course, if you real good, yuh go find ways of putting things in yuh conversation so yuh partner go get de hint. So, for instance if yuh talking 'bout how you see Manuel de grave digger, down de rumshop, dat might mean yuh have spades. Y'understand? Gravedigger, spades?

TOM. I'm liking that. Cracking codes, huh? You Brits are good at all that, ain't cha?

MANSION. I think we've got the first move, my love.

RUBY (*puts down a card*). Okay. How's that?

MANSION. Very nice, my dear.

TOM. So, Mansion, you must be a regular player. You up on all these quaint local customs, huh, 'old boy'?

MANSION. Oh yes, though I've not quite gone full native. The measure is, now, when a fly lands in my sundowner, I don't throw out the whole drink. But I still fish out the fly. Indeed, the islands do lend a certain flavour to all the old familiars, you'll find. Cricket for example, has almost been reinvented, the way they play it.

TOM. Baseball's my game.

MANSION. Oh no. You miss the point then, sir. Cricket's not a game. It's a philosophy. But you'd think it had always belonged to them, the way they play it. No Englishman would have thought he'd ever see the day we lost at Lords to a band of dark-skinned tourists.

DIAMOND *sings a line from 'Victory Test Match' by Lord Beginner.*

They've even elected a ruddy cricketer to government office. Constantine. Just imagine what's next.

TOM. Harry Belafonte for president?

TOM *laughs and* MANSION *chokes on his drink.*

MANSION. But it's a sign of good teaching when the student surpasses his master, so they say.

DIAMOND (*singing*). 'Ramadhin and Valentine.'

TOM. The son must slay the father and all that, huh?

MANSION. That's right, my boy. There's no fighting the natural order of things. One can only endeavour to sail with the prevailing wind.

DIAMOND. Tom, I go have to take yuh to see de Oval. Dat is we local cricket club. Is a set a high-rankin' officials and ting.

RUBY. They doh let in de ladies though.

TOM. Well. That's a shame.

DIAMOND. Nah, but all de big boys belonging to dat club. I have one or two contacts dat could get we in de clubhouse wid de big boys. Y'understand?

TOM *knows what* DIAMOND *is doing. He observes him and smiles.*

TOM. So how long have you been out here, Mansion?

MANSION. I came to prepare the way for the return journey of the Royal Tour of the colonies back in 1920. On this occasion, Young Edward, then the Prince of Wales, had voyaged as far as Australia, which of course required *The Renown*, his ship, to pass through the Panama Canal. Now, Trinidad is ideally located for a stopover en route. I Iiaised on that leg of the trip and you might say I liked the feel of the 'leg', so I stayed on.

RUBY (*sings*). 'I've danced with a man, Who's danced with a girl, Who's danced with the Prince of Wales!' (*She spills a bit of drink on her left breast and pats it dry.*) Oops. Look at that.

TOM. Hey, Edward the Prince, yes, I heard of him. We sold him the 'American Dream', didn't we. The Gay Divorcée. Edward and Mrs Simpson.

DIAMOND *sings a line from 'Love, Love Alone' by Harry Belafonte.*

MANSION. Indeed.

DIAMOND. Yuh see Edward? Like dat woman have he real tootoobay. Man, dem married woman. Nothing sweet like when you know is a next man own. A jealous husband? Kind of like mustard on your hotdog, eh Tom?

Yuh should ah see me, partner, back in Mayaro. Best, he was de boss man, de overseer. Big belly man, real soft, but he have dis real nice wife, when I tell yuh. When dat woman watch me, she speaking to me wid she eye, and she talking real loud.

MANSION *plays.*

Okay. I like the move, Mansion. Tom, watch dis one eh. It have plenty we go learn from he.

MANSION. How about you play your cards and lay off the old flannel, my boy.

DIAMOND. Ha, I know I ain't in your league, in de old boys' club.

DIAMOND *looks at* TOM.

TOM. So, this house, Alma, this where you used to live?

MANSION. Oh, for a time.

RUBY. Is just Pearl and me live here since I born.

MANSION. Well, Pearl has always been capable of running the business perfectly well and the arrangement has served me handsomely. If she sees it as her home, I know she'll look after its best interest.

RUBY. Well, it is her home. Is my home. I born right here.

MANSION. Indeed. Your mother has done a wonderful job making this house and an even better one making you, my dear. Two fine pieces of work.

RUBY *touches her heart and blows him a kiss.*

TOM. Such a shame you have intentions of leaving the island.

MANSION. Ha yes, the vultures are circling to claim the carcass of this old house.

TOM. Oh boy. We don't need all those vultures getting together. That's murder.

MANSION. That's crows, you'll find. A murder of crows. These Trinidadians call their vultures corbeaux. From the French, you see. But they're ugly things. Though beautiful in flight.

TOM. Is that so? Well, French, Trinidadian whatever they are, I like having a good old solid English fellow on the ground to keep things classy. It looks good for business.

MANSION. A sort of gentleman scarecrow? (TOM *laughs.*) Or are you really after this house for yourself? A circling bald eagle?

TOM. A bald eagle? I like that. But nope. I'm not looking for proprietorship. That's way too much responsibility. No, I certainly appreciate your loan of the space out back. I just wanna secure what happens once you weigh anchor.

DIAMOND. I tell yuh, Tom meh man, I go sort things out good. When Mansion gone you go be dealing wid we, partner.

TOM. Ah yes, kiddo. But there is the matter of Pearl running this place.

RUBY. Ha, and Pearl don't like no Yankees.

TOM. Which is a problem, frankly my dear. We'd be more comfortable with a more sympathetic party.

RUBY. That is why allyuh need we seeing over the things. Pearl ain't go make space for we, and she ain't go keep no Yankee business out back. You leave she in charge, next ting yuh know is PNM headquarters.

DIAMOND. Just sign we de deeds and everything going go sweet, Mansion. Rub meh belly ah go scratch yuh back.

MANSION. As inviting an offer as that may sound my boy, let's not get ahead of ourselves. Young American, you posture as your very own Roosevelt. With your very own Destroyers-for-Bases deal. I trust things are comfortable for you out in

Chagaramas. But you see now, I worked on that little pact and I know there's only so far one can trust agreements with allies. The ships the US sent to Churchill, in exchange for bases, were not fit for purpose.

TOM. Ah, but Uncle Sam came to the rescue. Again. If we didn't we wouldn't be sitting at this table playing this great game of All Fours.

MANSION. Dear boy, you and your Uncle had to. You'd joined the war.

TOM. Hey, Pearl Harbour was the line in the sand.

MANSION. Ha. Pearl Harbour makes great folklore. Folk News. Your Commander-In-Chief was already ordering attacks on enemy vessels in these waters. So much for your sanctified Neutrality Act. Pearl Harbour? You're thinking Hollywood. *From Here To Eternity*, Frank Sinatra. In fact, read the book instead, dear boy, it's much more honest. Hollywood has done a number on the American people with that movie.

TOM. Look now /

MANSION. But playing the martyr makes for a convenient backstory. Strategic. Then no level retaliation is too much, it can all be justified, even an atomic bomb.

TOM. Now, you listen /

MANSION. Come, come. We've been the best of bedfellows ever since. And now with that little attachment of yours grafted onto our 'backyard', there'll still be a good deal to harvest once I have retreated from these tropical jungles to the bucolic pastures of dear old Blighty.

RUBY. But who you leavin' in charge? Coz peg-leg Pearl not going to give you no bumper crop. That woman hand 'tight like chicken bamsie'.

DIAMOND. Well, we go see to all ah dat. All I's askin' is dat I could get a little piece ah de action on de side. A little someting I could move here for you. In a local market.

TOM. Nice try, but 'fraid not buddy.

DIAMOND. 'Fraid not what?

TOM. Any stock is already accounted for, I told you. Now listen, anything found to have gone missing, my friend, could prove, well, fatal might sound a bit strong, but well hey, it'd be accurate.

RUBY. What kind of thing you storing out there?

TOM. Oh beauty, don't you worry that pretty, little head. It's the best way for you to keep it.

DIAMOND. Well, I was only wondering if it have some few nice American supplies I could find a market for meself. Just a little something for yuh boy.

TOM. American supplies? What, ketchup? Cigarettes? Oh, that's a good one. Diamond, you want some cigarettes, we'll see what we can do for you.

DIAMOND. Well, I wasn't tinking dat necessarily… I more interested in what yuh have holding up out back.

TOM. And that's not for you. You leave that alone. We gotta be able to trust you, little buddy. We don't want our suppliers getting uneasy.

DIAMOND. But how yuh mean? It must have a little something dere for we. Dis is we house. You cah just use it as allyuh backyard and all we getting is some old cigarette. Wha' de arse is dat?

MANSION. Might I advise you, dear boy, to take advantage of the cigarette offer and keep well away from the rest. Unless I can feel assured of your cooperation, we shall have to remove the obstacle completely.

RUBY *coughs and puts her hands to her chest, indicating her heart.* TOM *observes her, but* MANSION *is caught up with* DIAMOND.

DIAMOND. De 'obstacle'. Who, me? I is de obstacle now? Me one? Is me alone gettin' threaten' here but you willing to have de whole US navy storing tings in your backyard? Is who run tings here?

RUBY *takes* MANSION*'s glass and goes over to the bar.*

MANSION. Ironic, yes, it is. But when I first met you, my lad, you yourself pointed out to me the permanence of our American friends. 'To beguile the time, look like the time'. A threat from one man can be dealt with. Easy. You get rid of the man. A threat from a force, such as our American friends here, that's all together different. That you have to deal with. Negotiate. 'Bear welcome in your eye, your hand, your tongue.'

DIAMOND. But is me what… Yuh cyah just…

MANSION. It's your play, son.

RUBY *returns with a bottle and a glass which she hands to* MANSION. *He sips and sputters. He looks at his glass then at* RUBY *who gives a small smile and hands him the bottle.*

RUBY. Diamond, come nuh man. Take de cigarettes and done. Relax. Yuh soundin' desperate. That ain't have no class.

TOM. Deals come and go my friend, but some things are forever. (*Smiles*)

MANSION. 'Look like the innocent flower but be the serpent under it.' Diamond, may I suggest that you follow your sister's advice, she seems to catch on very quickly.

DIAMOND *puts down a card.* RUBY *plays next.*

RUBY *sings the opening line of 'Rum and Coca-Cola' by the Andrews Sisters.*

TOM. Andrews Sisters, nice.

DIAMOND. Andrew Sisters my backside. Dat is Lord Invader write dem lyrics.

TOM *plays and* DIAMOND *lets out a gasp.* MANSION *plays his final card.*

MANSION. And there we have it.

TOM. Is that 'game over'?

RUBY *squeals, jumps from her chair and slaps her cards on the table.*

RUBY. High, low, high, low, Jack to go. Boy, like dey 'Hang yuh Jack'.

DIAMOND. What? Why yuh play dat? Wha' you doin'?

TOM. Hey man, I told yuh I had diamonds. You know: 'some things are forever'? You weren't paying attention.

DIAMOND. Diamonds? Yuh ain't get me telling you clubs de whole time. Clubs. Cricket clubs, old boys' clubs.

TOM. Golly, were you telling me something with all that stuff? Gee, I didn't get that.

MANSION. Well, my little Mata Hari over there, I thought it strange you suddenly switched my tipple. But 'Harts', very clever.

RUBY. Well, what I go do if you too busy arguing to see meh signals?

TOM. Hey, is that right, Rube? You did that? Beauty and brilliance. Dangerous combination. I like that.

DIAMOND. My arse! We were winning that. I had de blasted jack. You must ah throw de game on purpose, if yuh ask me.

TOM. Hey, take it easy pal. It's only a game.

MANSION *rising from his chair and taking his hat.*

MANSION. That's the difference my friend. You Americans play games and we British enjoy our sports but this lot play everything like life or death. It's vulgar but hugely entertaining. Don't you think? Ruby, we can partner any day you like, my precious. Young American, long may our special arrangement yield happy returns.

RUBY *kisses* MANSION*'s cheek and walks with him to the door.*

TOM. Mansion, pleasure doing business with you. Best game of Bridge I ever played.

MANSION *laughs and exits* TOM *puts 'Matilda' by Harry Belafonte back on.*

Hearts. Fantastic. That's a class move, Rube. Valuable team player. I gotta remember that one. Here baby, this one's for you.

Diamond, we gotta play that again. Baby, I'm bushed. Let's call it a night. You ready to join me?

RUBY. You staying here tonight?

TOM. Babe, that game's got me all heated and bothered and I reckon you got what I need to cool me down.

TOM *kisses* RUBY *as* DIAMOND *looks on.*

Diamond, I'll look into those cigarettes in the morning. See what we can do for you, fella. You coming, Ruby?

TOM *exits.*

RUBY *and* DIAMOND *look at each other as Harry sings.*

Eventually RUBY *exits after* TOM.

DIAMOND *sits on his own for a bit then gets up and exits to the back of the house.*

The stage is empty as we listen to the music.

DIAMOND *comes in lifting a heavy crate. He carries it with difficulty across the stage. He exits through the street door. The song finishes. Sound of the record spinning on the turntable.*

Lights down.

Scene Two

RUBY *is alone. She moves one of the chairs over to a large cupboard at the back of the room. She opens the cupboard door and stands on the chair.*

She struggles to reach down an attractive valise.

She doesn't see SELDOM *enter in his police uniform. He observes her for a moment.*

SELDOM *sings verse from 'Sweet Like A Honey Bee'.*

RUBY *is startled but covers it well as she gets down with the valise. During the following she discreetly stashes it, closes the cupboard and returns the chair.*

RUBY. Oh my God, well is a whole set ah Jab devil in de place now. Watch who reach back.

SELDOM. So, what yuh sayin' dahlin? Yuh miss me?

RUBY. Why? You been gone somewhere?

SELDOM. Aye yie yie, doux-doux dahlin'. You know I love it when you treat meh bad. You have to say true doh, yuh purse at least must be miss me. Doh from the welcome sight I got as I walk in, yuh purse is de only ting dat growing lean.

RUBY (*steupses*). My purse is as healthy as what you lookin' at.

SELDOM. Jeez 'n' ages, you must be the queen ah England with a purse dat big.

RUBY. Boy stop yuh stupidness. You want a drink?

SELDOM. Gimme something, nuh.

RUBY. What yuh want? Whisky, bourbon?

SELDOM. Bur-who? But what happen to yuh mudder rum?

RUBY. It have dat. You want dat.

SELDOM. Well, gimme dat.

As RUBY *gets the drink,* DIAMOND *enters from the street.* DIAMOND *carries a 'Salvatori Scott and Co' shopping bag. Spotting* SELDOM *in uniform,* DIAMOND *pauses before coming in.*

Ay partner, you aright?

DIAMOND. Aright.

SELDOM. You lookin' for someting?

RUBY (*with the drink*). Yuh ain't meet me brother?

SELDOM. Brother? You have brother?

RUBY. Buh wha' happen to you? Why I can't have brother?

SELDOM. Coz, wherever you come out from girl, dey only make de one ah you. (*To* DIAMOND.) No offence, brother. Hold on. I just get it. From last time I was here. You was delivering them crate ah rum and ting. Not so?

RUBY. Ay. But you know is true. I forget. That delivery from Mahadeo.

PEARL *emerges from the back room.*

PEARL. Ay-ay, Seldom? Dat is you? How you been gone so long?

SELDOM *gets to his feet and goes to kiss* PEARL.

SELDOM. Lord, Miss Pearl. My eyes miss yuh. Dey had me way down South.

RUBY. What you doin' back here. De road finish build?

SELDOM. As if! Nah, child, dey have we back here looking for some man. Miss Pearl, who dis I now meeting? Dis is yuh son?

PEARL. Aw, him. Yes.

SELDOM. Lord, Miss Pearl, yuh trying to make me jealous. I did always tink I was a son to you.

PEARL *steupses and laughs. She sees* DIAMOND*'s shopping bag.*

PEARL. Wha' dat?

DIAMOND. Here, I have something for yuh. I buy yuh a present.

PEARL *is taken aback.*

Open de box, see wha' I get yuh.

PEARL *takes a box out of the bag and opens it.*

She takes out and observes the finely cobbled pair of shoes.

Is a proper pair of walking shoe so yuh doh have to mash up yuh foot when yuh does be walking all over Port of Spain. What yuh tink?

SELDOM (*whistles*). Boy dat is a fine set ah shoe. Where yuh buy dat? It must be real money yuh have.

DIAMOND. Nah man. A fella can't just watch he mudder breaking she foot everyday. Man, wid dat shoe she could walk from here to Galeota Point.

DIAMOND *sings a line from 'Old lady walk a mile and a half' by Lord Kitchener.*

SELDOM. Galeota Point… Dat is in Mayaro not so?

DIAMOND. Yuh doh like de shoe or what? How you not sayin' nothing?

SELDOM. Well, dat is a hell of a ting.

DIAMOND. What?

SELDOM. Well, de man dey send we back here to find, dat I was just telling dem 'bout, he from Mayaro.

DIAMOND. Man?

SELDOM. Eh heh. Dey say he is a real badjohn. He was workin' on de road dem Americans makin', but dis fella like to big up himself and gamble with the foreman and big boys down there. Well, de foreman, he name Best, dis saga boy real get under Best skin 'cause of how he like to pull ah set ah old style, strutting around in he fancy dandan like nobody cah touch he. Best vex, so every day he give dis badjohn all de shit job, hard labour and sweat, work he like a dog. But every night, de fella turning up smelling sweet and looking spiff and gambling wid big money. So Best eye turn bad and he set he up to lose, and de badjohn end up owing serious money to dem big boys down south. And dem is local mafia, yuh doh be messin' wid dem gangstahs. Y'understan?

So, check it now, next ting yuh know a whole set of money gone missin' from Best office and de American bosses send for de police. Somebody thief de payroll. Best get lock up. Well, when Best get out de people jail, he gone home and he only cussing dis badjohn name. Me cah remember what he called… something, something.

Anyway, now, Best have a wife. Dey say she does move like water. Now when Best getting so obsessed wid dis badjohn, screamin' out he name in he sleep and all, like Best wife get mad how he only running down dis man. Devil take she and de woman gone and tell Best how dis badjohn does be fuckin' she good and proper for de longest while. And how Best so stupid, he feel he giving dis fella horrors at work but de two ah dem does only be laughing at he stupid arse. How is she what take de payroll money and give it to dis badjohn, what he name, cause 'she love him', 'he more man dan Best go ever be', 'especially in bed'. Whoo papa. Who tell she say dat? Best beat she arse. Woman still in hospital all now.

So now is Best, de mafia, police, everybody looking for dis badjohn. A set ah bacchanal! I tell yuh dis. See me? I is police and I go tell yuh he only have to pray is de police what find him first. 'Cause if is mafia what find him, dey going take turns killing he and me ain't know how many times a man could die. Dey does say is just de once, but me ain't tink so, nuh. I see dese fellas work already. It have plenty ways to die.

PEARL *puts the shoes on the table, stands and leaves the room.*

Oh lawd, watch de time. Ruby girl, I gone. Apparently dey feel dis fella reach quite here in Port of Spain. Wha' yuh name again?

DIAMOND. Diamond.

SELDOM. Oh yes, Diamond. Alright I go see yuh partner. Ruby, tell Miss Pearl I gone.

SELDOM *exits. Long silence.* DIAMOND *eventually pours himself a drink.*

RUBY. One for de road then?

DIAMOND. Eh?

RUBY. One for de road? I figure you go be leavin' about now? (DIAMOND *doesn't answer.*) Boy your arse cook. Time to jump off de fire.

DIAMOND. Why I should leave? Where I goin' to go?

RUBY. Me ain't know but you need to go real soon. It have a price on your head.

DIAMOND. Doh mind dat. I have money. I go pay dem. As for Best, he could kiss meh arse. Since I small I work on de estate every day; plodding round in cow shit in meh jigger boots, sweating an' flinging cutlass, but dat kinda sweat yuh cah ever wash off and when yuh pass next to all dem big man and dey fancy woman you see dem curl dey mouth and pull up dey nose 'cause you does smell bad. I say ain't me in no set ah cowshit again. But when dem people see me trying to be free, dey don't like it and I land up in jail. And is sweat I still sweating but now I in jail and dey chain me up. And when I get out de fuckin' jail, is de same sweat and de same road dey have me wukkin' and I realise I ain't never goin' be free. So, when Best want to treat me like I is beast, I only watch he and laugh coz is de beast wid two back dat I makin' wid he wife every night.

RUBY. How yuh mean you go pay them? Is what set of money you have so?

DIAMOND. Doh mind 'bout money. See dis house here? You and me girl, we go run dis place like de King and Queen ah Port of Spain.

RUBY. 'We'? You come from quite Mayaro and want tell me what to do in dis house? Some Mayaro country-bookie.

DIAMOND. How you mean? You is from Mayaro.

RUBY. I beg your pardon? I ain't from no blasted Mayaro. I born Port of Spain.

DIAMOND. And where your mudder from? Not Mayaro?

RUBY. To hell wid dat. I born here. Dat woman may have given birth to you but she ain't no mother. She get rid of you a long time ago. You ain't have no right here at all.

DIAMOND. Ruby, why you just turn so? I tell you already, is you an' me. We does work good together, Ruby. Everything I want is for you. (DIAMOND *approaches* RUBY *and touches her face.*) It's all for you.

RUBY. For me, my eye. You just want to save your arse.

DIAMOND. No. I doh understand. What happen? You know is you I want. Is you I need.

PEARL *walks into the room unseen as* DIAMOND *kisses* RUBY. RUBY *then pushes him away.*

(*Shows her the money.*) Rubes, doh worry. As long as dem people doin' business in we backyard we must be alright. A share of dat must belong to we. Dey ain't even goin' miss dis. We just keep dem sweet and everything go be good.

RUBY. You tief something from in de back?

DIAMOND. I just take a little bit of what was in dem crate. My share. Not enough for dem to notice. But enough so dat I could pay off dem mafia boss and you and I could be free like breeze.

RUBY. Me? I done free already. I like it so. You and your stupidness go lose we everything. 'I hear bigger cock dan you crow and still land up in de pot.'

They spot PEARL. *She is wearing her old pair of shoes.*

DIAMOND. What yuh doin? Why you doh wear yuh new shoe?

PEARL. You need to be going. You take your damn shoe and leave.

DIAMOND. How you mean?

PEARL. When dose men find you, you best not be in dis house. Dis old house tired. Dis house see enough bacchanal and confusion.

DIAMOND. So, what dat have to do wid me?

PEARL. You bringing your badness in here for me to deal wid. Telling me about angels, how you come to find that piece what been missing all dese years. My arse. You come in here to save yuh backside. Giving me a whole set of guilt. Trumpin' wid de guilt card so I cah tell you nothing and just have to watch you move yuhself in, into my house, my life, when I done get rid ah you so long ago.

DIAMOND. I ain't giving you no set ah guilt. I come for me mudder. Everybody have a mudder. Why, me so, why I cah have none?

PEARL. Exploitation, you come here for. Well, I have enough ah dat, thank you. English man, American man. Doh feel dat I get fool, cause your face black I cah see you exploiting de same way. What it is you really come here for? Is money you want to save your stupid sorry skin? You come here to tief de roof from over my head?

DIAMOND. I ain't looking to tief. I is yuh firstborn son. I's a man, I must claim what is mines. I supposed to do dat. How I go be a man if you doh let me?

PEARL. You doh get permission to be man. Doh come in here smelling yuhself and tell me you is man. You ain't nothing.

DIAMOND. If I is nothing is you what make me so. What kind of woman does give way she child? Even bitch-dog in de road doh do dat. Doh mind if dat pothound starving and weak, you come near she child, she go bite yuh hand off. But you, you just send me way. Dat ain't natural. But dat is de legacy I get. I come here looking for birthright and all I get is pure legacy.

PEARL. Birthright? You feel you is some kind ah lord or what? I suffer my whole life for dis house. It cost me plenty. For what? For you? For she? De only thing I done wrong is to make children dat not worth nothing.

RUBY. Old woman, you's kill me yuh know. You doh even have no rights in yuh own house. Keep it. Who want it? The way you does talk 'bout dis house you woulda swear it was Buckingham Palace. Dis crumbling down little piece ah shit.

PEARL. You shut yuh nasty mouth, you little jamette. I see you, yuh know. Wid yuh nastiness. Yuh own brudder. But you was always so. I should ah sew you up when you was a child. From de time you small, as soon as all dem man would reach, you used to come in here wearing just vest and panty and come sit on dey lap so dey go give you present and ting. I shoulda sew you up. I give you everyting. I build dis house. I break meh bones. So you could go to school and be decent. And watch you now. You are such a disappointment to me.

RUBY. Doh even try it old woman. Is who bring dose men in de house so I coulda sit on dey lap? Is you who choose the record. Doh try and blame de gramophone if you doh like de tune.

PEARL. I shame. I shame to see what I bring in de world. Good for nothing, worthless, weak fools. When I reach back, I want both ah allyuh gone.

RUBY. Or what? Let me hear you try tell Mansion you make me leave, see what he say. And dis weak-arse son you make here, he go dead just now. Being born from dat belly, dat's as good as a death sentence. Dat womb cursed.

PEARL *slaps* RUBY.

(*Stick-fighters' chant.*) 'Mooma. Mooma. Yuh son in de grave aready, yuh son in de grave aready. Take a towel and ban' yuh belly.'

TOM *has entered and observes the proceedings.*

TOM. Well, this is a stirring family scene. Very Norman Rockwell.

DIAMOND. Hey man. How yuh doin'? We wasn't expectin' you dis evening.

TOM. Ha, yes. I come with news. I'm being shipped out in the morning, my dear.

RUBY. You leaving now?

TOM We're heading to South America. Hey, shoes on the table. Now that's bad luck, isn't it? Wow, but they're pretty something huh? Nice.

DIAMOND. Dem is Pearl shoe.

RUBY. When you go reach back?

TOM. Well, we'll be sending more supplies back here to be stored but no telling who'll be running our side of things in the future.

Hey, Pearl? These are pretty good. Where'd you get these? Salvatori? I gotta take a look see if I can get me some.

DIAMOND. Well, is me what buy dem for she.

TOM. Wow. Really?

DIAMOND. Yeah. You know, a man cah watch he mudder squeeze up she foot in de same old shoe de whole time.

TOM. I like that. You're right. A boy's got to look after his momma. You're a lucky woman, Pearl. Must've cost you a few greenbacks.

RUBY. Why you doh ask him where he get de money.

TOM. What's that?

RUBY. Dem is big time, fancy import. Italian. Dat not cheap yuh know. You should ask he where he get the money.

TOM. Oh. Right. Really?

DIAMOND. Doh watch dat man. So, who we go be dealin' wid down here if you goin'?

RUBY. He buyin' foreign shoe. You ain't goin' ask him where he get de money?

TOM. Alright then. Where?

DIAMOND. Ruby?

RUBY. Well, I know allyuh is big time businessman and whatnot so you must have a inventory and ting right? Well maybe you should go out in de back and do some stock takin'.

TOM. Say again.

RUBY. 'You put fowl to watch corn.'

DIAMOND. Ruby? Wha' you doin'? Wah' you sayin'?

TOM. Okay. I think I get you. Damn. Diamond, my good friend, you're one hell of a guy, ain't yuh. Cojones. You wanna fill me in?

DIAMOND. I ain't take nothing much. Just what should be mine. Reparation, brudder. All yuh wheelin' and dealin' but is me doin' de work for yuh and is my mudder house you using to do it in. We in dis. You cah just pay we a set ah cigarette and dat is it. But watch, I make good money for it, yuh know. You just need to bring me in on dis ting.

TOM. Oh Diamond, Diamond, Diamond. Tell me it ain't so. You do not have a part in all of this. We can't let the animals run the farm. Your little house is just a stop over, a piss stop.

DIAMOND. Dis is we home, not no damn latrine.

PEARL. You get out me house. I not havin' this shit in my house. Get out.

DIAMOND. Ma… ma. Take it easy.

PEARL. Who de hell you callin' 'Ma'? Is you bring dis prospector in my damn house. Taking it over piece by piece. A bit from de back, a bit from de side. All ah yawl taking what is mine right from under me.

RUBY. Oh, hush up. None of this belongs to you. None.

TOM. Hey lady. I'm sorry you're taking that there stance on matters. It's not a good look. You don't realise how lucky you are that Mansion and my good self are even interested in this old place.

PEARL. We don't need you here. None ah yawl. Allyuh two chupidee feel you wheelin' and dealin'. For what? Where's yuh substance? What you go have left when these new masters done wid you? Look for a next teet to suck. And it ain't go never change. It go always be Rediffusion rental mentality, till it's all frittered away and dey holding yuh purse.

TOM. So, you going to go it alone, Madam Pearl? Or you forming a union of belligerents somewhere?

PEARL. Well, allyuh devils form allyuh unions. United States, United Kingdom…

TOM. Ha, your Williams, the noise he makes may please you now but he's no match for Uncle Sam.

PEARL. It ain't just Eric Williams, tings changing. India, Ghana, de rest ah dem. You watch. That wind blowing like is kite season.

TOM. Haha. That ain't gonna last, honey. Once your little hero goes from being a sprat in the oceans of Empire to a shark in your little sea, he'll get a taste for power. There'll be no union. Do you think he can even unite this country? You people? Then you will be all on your lonesome, and you'll remember that it's actually been our backyard that you've been living in all this time. And we don't have room for anyone who's not with us. So, watch your back, lady.

RUBY. Tom, doh mind she. She cah do nothing to nobody. It have bigger fish frying.

TOM. Diamond, kiddo. We can't have messy little people like you dipping your sticky little thumbs into the pie. Where's the cash?

DIAMOND. I got it man. It's all here.

He hands over the cash.

TOM. What's this? How much did you get this for? What did you take?

DIAMOND. Just one crate.

TOM. One crate. Goddamn, kiddo. This is all you got? For a whole crate?

DIAMOND. Well, except for de shoe. But doh worry, I got de receipt.

TOM. Aw man. You are priceless. Where'd you take the goods, man? You gotta get them back.

DIAMOND. Mmm, nah. Dese fellas way up in de hills dere. Yuh ain't going find dem.

TOM (*attacks the furniture*). WHAT? WHAT WHAT WHAT WHAT?

(*Stops. Is he going to cry?*) Arrrhhhh, I'm dead. I'm fucking dead.

Silence. Gathers himself.

So, listen. I'm not going to lie to you. This is a big mess. And I'm not sticking my neck out for some village idiot who can't keep his dick in his pants. So, here's the deal. You come with me now. We go see my commander. He's a reasonable guy, he'll sort it out. This is his sideline you see. Below the radar.

DIAMOND. But hear nuh…

TOM. No, no, no. You just tell it to the Commander like you told it to me. All about the house, and reparation, don't leave that bit out.

DIAMOND. But…

TOM. Don't forget the cash. And hey, why don't you bring the shoes. I think that'll be a great prop for the show-and-tell. You got the receipt? Don't look so scared. It's not reassuring.

TOM *holds open the front door.*

Ruby, we'll do farewells when I come back to check the merchandise. Pearl.

TOM *exits with* DIAMOND *and the shoes in their bag.*

RUBY *looks at* PEARL. *She covers her terror with an air of defiance and retrieves the valise as she rushes to the back of the house.*

PEARL *watches her leave. She turns back to the front door. Eventually she takes a chair and moves it to sit watching the door in silence.*

Lights fade. There is a hiss and a spark as the bulb blows.

Scene Three

Nighttime in the house. PEARL *has lit a lamp.*

The room is dark and empty. Silence.

We hear the sound of fumbling and then a collapse outside the front door.

The door opens and we see DIAMOND *crumpled on the floor, hanging onto the door knob.*

He has been badly beaten and is clearly in a lot of pain and great distress.

He locks the door and then crawls into the room. PEARL *comes in and finds him weeping on the floor.*

She bends over towards him but seems unsure what to do.

PEARL. I been waiting for you to reach back. Is who do this to yuh?

DIAMOND *tries to stand and collapses again with the pain.*

Here, doh try and move.

PEARL *goes to the bar and gets a towel and a bowl of water. She brings over a bottle of rum and a glass. She pours some rum and hands it to* DIAMOND. *She gets down onto the floor with him, wets the towel and tentatively wipes some of the blood from his face.*

DIAMOND *drinks the rum and cries softly as she cleans his face.* DIAMOND *reaches out and holds* PEARL *then buries his face in her lap and sobs.*

DIAMOND *takes her hand and puts it on his head. She strokes him.*

DIAMOND. Touch me. Please. Touch my head. When I was a chile I used to make you up in meh mind and when I used to cry I would bury meh face like dis. And you had dis big soft lap and you would hold me and I could just hide in there.

Dey hurt me, Ma. I sorry. I's sorry I's not a man. They done kill me.

PEARL. Who do this? Where you been whole night?

DIAMOND. On de ship. Down in de base. They grab meh soul from straight out meh body, Ma.

PEARL. What dey do yuh?

DIAMOND. How you going to ask me dat? How you go watch me like dis and ask me dat? So what? So you could tell me I weak, I not a man and I shame yuh. Well fuck you. Where de Hell you was? I used to watch all dem other children in de school. Dey mudder would dress dem nice-nice so. Morning time you see dem coming in smelling sweet, sweet coz dey mudder bathe dem and you could see dem wid de white talcum powder all up by dey neck where dey mudder powder dem down like fish for frying. They reach in school wid dey uniform clean and crisp. You could ah smell it; smell how much dey mudder love dem. Smell it in de heat from de iron on dey clothes, smell it in de sweet talc and de carbolic soap. In de hair grease shining on dey head. And when lunchtime come dey used to run home for dey hot food. But when dey reach back in de school I would beat dem.

Beat dem coz dey belly full and it make dem slow and lazy. Beat dem coz I know when the teacher gimme licks it go make me forget de hole in meh belly and de pain in me head.

I come here and I find you and yuh ain't even tell meh why. Why yuh wasn't dere, why you never hold meh hand, or scratch meh head, or cook meh rice, or beat meh when I break de window playin' cricket in de yard. Why you wasn't dere to tell me 'bout me granfadder and where he was born and how he brave and tall and strong and how I go grow up and be just like he, coz I is a good boy and you make me and love me and how yuh go die before yuh let anybody hurt me. But dey hurt me, Ma. Dey hurt meh bad. And you wasn't fucking there.

DIAMOND *has moved away.* PEARL *goes to him. She strokes his head and pours him another drink.*

PEARL (*sings*). 'Safasa mama
Maliweh
Saki batni mama
bweniwe
Indeh Salmana
Safasa Mama
Maliwe'

Beat.

Nobody had told me it was forever. What I did wasn't wrong. Dat is what people did den. It was how we used to live. Other people does leave dey child. But I didn't realise how far it was going to be. I didn't realise that whole worlds could come between us and I would never see my child again. I had to tell meself yuh wasn't meh child no more, dat your life belong to someone else now. I had to lie to stop de pain. Dis unnatural pain. And dey used to watch me. De people in town and say 'see she, she give 'way she child. I hear dat woman have baby and she just gone and leave he'. And you was a beautiful child. Oh. When you born, I just watch you and I feel 'dis child cah come from me and look so'. If I couldn't ah remember my blood on your face and de cord tying yuh belly to my own, I wouldn't have believe dat is me what make you. All de neighbours used to fight to take turn to hold you. But I did know you was mine. I thought I would have come get yuh. But de people who keep yuh say no, dey ain't sending you to live in badness with me. And everybody say to me that your life go be better off widdout me. And de shame and de guilt… After a while it come like you dead. And den I had to tell meself I must be lose meh mind. I must be never had no child, coz how I could ah have a child and me ain't never go see he again?

I feel like you dead coz dat was easier dan de hurtin' inside to feel I give 'way meh own child.

When you reach in here and I see yuh, I know I could feel something, I could feel de force of a whole world that never was. Never had a chance to be. But when you stand up in front of me, it was like if I watch you, you go make me see mehself. So I tell meself no. Dis man is not my child. I lost a little boy and I don't know why dis big man want to stand in front of me and make me see mehself.

You still feelin' pain son?

There is heavy knocking on the front door. Someone tries to open it. It's locked. More banging.

DIAMOND *tries to struggle to his feet.* PEARL *helps to pull him up.* RUBY *comes out from the back and sees them.*

RUBY *is fully dressed in a smart travel suit. There is another knock and* RUBY *goes to open the door.* SELDOM *enters.*

RUBY. Boy what you doin' here banging on de door so?

SELDOM. Ruby… Oh, Miss Pearl, goodnight-goodnight.

(SELDOM *observes* DIAMOND.) Like something gone on here already. I must be come late.

RUBY. No. I don't think so. What yuh mean?

SELDOM. What happen to he?

PEARL. Don't you mind him. Dat is man business. Is what you doin' here?

SELDOM. Me ain't staying, doh mind dat. Ruby girl, you and I goin' back a long way, so I feel I cah just leave you so and not let yuh know dat it go be big trouble here tonight. I had was to warn yuh.

Dis fella, yuh brudder, everybody looking for he. But somebody somewhere fix it so dat de police ain't go find he until after dem gangsta man done finish wid him and get dey payback. Dat is why I watch he now and I want to know if dey done find him already. But nah. He ain't go be standing so, drinking no rum if dese fellas had find he. Not dem fellas. Miss Pearl, hear nuh, I have a lot a respect for you. You look out for me since I small. Me ain't want see a set ah killin' and commess in your house. Dis place go be pure pandemonium tonight. Yes partner, 'if I lie, I die'. Folks, I gone.

RUBY *looks round at* DIAMOND.

RUBY. What happen to you?

DIAMOND. Ask yuh man what happen to me. Where he?

PEARL. Diamond, come, leave de house now. You have to go.

RUBY. You best leave for true. 'Crapaud smoke yuh pipe', boy. Dem fellas goin' kill you dead.

DIAMOND. Leh dem come. What you care? Is you what go and do dis to me.

RUBY. Me? I do what?

DIAMOND. Is you what go tell yuh American. Why? Why Ruby? Why you do me dis? I love you.

RUBY. 'Cockroach have no business in fowl party'. Who you feel you messin' wid? If you so mad dat you want to get yuhself kill, dat is you. But you dangerous to have around. When dey ketch you, all ah we go pay.

DIAMOND. I'd ah look after you. All I care about is you.

RUBY. Care about me? Who is you? I don't need you to care about me. You best care 'bout yuhself and get de hell outta here.

DIAMOND. I can't leave.

RUBY. Boy, you crazy?

PEARL. Is why you dress like dat? Where you goin' at all?

RUBY. I leavin'. When Tom come back, he go have to take me too.

DIAMOND. Stay here, stay wid me. Yuh cah see or what? Dis ting, whatever it is dat bring you and me together now, is because I was meant to find yuh.

Dis ting pull meh here so hard it hurt like I just born. My life doh make no sense widout you.

RUBY. You's a mad arse. I ain't mad like you. If you feel I want to stay here and die in dis hellhole wid you den you wrong. I savin' myself. You too stupid to even run.

DIAMOND. I go look after you.

RUBY. You cah look after nobody. You dead already. You spend yuh whole life lyin' and tiefin' and blamin' everybody else for all your stupidness and your waste. Nothing more sad than a wasted life. Anything dat doh grow is dead. But you see me, I alive and I movin' on. And now I have dis next ting growin' inside ah me and if I stay here is both ah we dead. I have to save my own life if I go save dis child.

DIAMOND. Child?

RUBY. Yes. But you doh study that.

DIAMOND. We havin' a child?

RUBY. 'We' who? Who is 'we'? This child goin' to save me and he both. And I getting my arse de hell outta here. Tonight.

DIAMOND. Don't go.

RUBY. Nah, nah. Once Tom find out I havin' he child he cah just leave me here. And I ain't waiting here to see what go born. Cause if dis ting born and it look like you den dat is all ah we dead. Death sentence.

DIAMOND. How yuh mean?

RUBY. You can't see or what? It's the same damn thing over and over again. My choice is what? Stay here in downtown hell and bring up dis child to do de same shit, play de same

Old Mas on de streets of Port of Spain. Or what? Go off and leave it like how she do you? Den is de same shit again. De same pain dat pass on throughout de generations like blood. Like how big foot or fat bottom pass down in de family. Well not me and dat. I breakin' dat chain. I gone. I savin' my child. And if it cost your life to save my child den dat is what it cost.

PEARL. Diamond, please. I just get back meh son and my whole life like he was dead. Doh hear she with she badness. Boy you alive. And yuh did come back to yuh mudder. Doh go and dead now. Here, wait…

PEARL *goes over to the wooden sculpture and struggles to unbolt it from its plinth.*

DIAMOND. If I run now, what kinda man is dat. If I not a man, I ain't nothing. I doh exist. What? I find I have child and I must run? It have a child in there and that is you and me.

DIAMOND *touches* RUBY*'s stomach tenderly.*

RUBY. This is not your child.

DIAMOND. If is chain you want to break is only love go break it. When a child born and it know dat it loved real bad, you ever see what dat does look like? Dat go break all de chain it have.

DIAMOND *kisses* RUBY. *As they embrace,* PEARL *lifts the heavy wooden sculpture onto the table.* RUBY *draws away.*

PEARL. Diamond, help me here, son. Come help me open dis box here.

RUBY. You spend yuh whole life crying nobody ain't love yuh. How all of a sudden you is a expert?

DIAMOND. I love you. You could teach me.

RUBY. Dis ain't love. Dis is just some kind of sickness.

If they doh kill you, I go kill you myself. Because you're weak…

DIAMOND. I'm strong enough to love you. To love dis child.

RUBY. Dead man can't be no father. If I let you near my child, he go be dead like you.

TOM *comes through the front door.*

TOM. Diamond. Wow. You made it back. Well. Most people don't even stand up too good after they been to see the Commander.

DIAMOND. You know what they was goin' do to me?

TOM. I had a fair idea. It's not my kind of thing, personally. You might be a good-looking guy but I don't really got the stomach for it. But the Commander, he's a whole different human. When he gets enraged, it kind of gets him going. He gets pretty nasty though, don't he?

PEARL (*understanding*). Son. Oh God.

TOM. Hey man, here you are. You're still alive. That's the bright side. Trick now is to stay alive.

DIAMOND (*spirit is coming to him*). Nah. Ting now is to die a man. My whole life dey treat me like a boy, a animal and den dey lock me up and dey treat me like a beast. And de more dey see dat I can take all de pain and I still growing strong and proud and I still beautiful – And de more dey watch in my eye is de more dey 'fraid what dey see cause dey look at me but dey see demself and so they want to cut me down. Like you so tonight. But it doh help you to kill me, coz den I just dead and you just livin'. But you make me into a beast and that make you into a man. You need me.

Well tonight I feel pain, more pain dan I ever feel. Not when whip lash me or boot kick me or knife cut me. Dis pain wrench meh whole soul from inside me. Now for true, I dead. What I running for? To live and be like dem jumbie dat you does see on de road. Madness in dey eye, looking to find where dey leave dey spirit. Like a soucouyant at sunrise looking under every stone for where she leave she skin.

DIAMOND *pulls out a knife and squares up to* TOM.

TOM. Wonderful. Diamond. Hey, you're just as the name says. But listen buddy, I ain't got have a whole bunch of time. So, thanks for the speech but I'm just gonna get straight to the point.

TOM *pulls out a revolver and points it at* DIAMOND.

US Navy issue, my friend. So, let's just put down the knife. Don't worry. I don't take it personally. Just put down the knife and it's all over.

DIAMOND *continues towards* TOM *with the knife.*

I understand. A man can get very confused after the Commander takes his payment. But that's the cost of staying alive for you, my friend. That's what you got wrong. You can't afford pride. The price is too high and you been borrowing your whole life.

RUBY. Tom, leh we go. I comin' wid you. Let we leave now.

TOM. Now why would you be coming with me, sweetcakes?

RUBY. It have a future growing here inside me. One we makin' together. I ain't staying here for the past to kill me. And kill the only chance we got.

TOM. Now what's that? Chance for what? Diamond, put down that knife. This is not the time for games, my son – (*Places his gun down within reach on the table.*) See, no gun. Just put it down. / Put it down.

RUBY. Tom, we got to go, man. I have to come with you. Take me on your ship, put me on a plane, / I could come meet you.

PEARL (*still struggling with the plinth*). Diamond put down the knife. Come help me here, son.

DIAMOND. Dat ting in yuh belly ain't leavin'. Is here it stayin. If de devil waitin for me, I go see he in hell but you ain't goin' nowhere.

TOM. He's lost his ever-loving mind! /

RUBY. Tom, pick up de gun and leh we go. De man crazy… / You can't leave me here.

DIAMOND (*taken by spirit, speaking in 'Midnight Robber' style*). But while I here on dis God's earth I shall rise up. Yes, they thought they had vanquished me but I done dead and gone to Hell and Lucifer take me and show me de mountain ranges and de valleys and say 'behold all dis shall be yours'. But I know the Devil speaks with forked tongues and I rebuke him here. God speaks to me and acknowledges me as his son and promises me redemption for my sins and for his sweet glory must I slay Beelzebub or his reign of evil shall spread plague and pestilence to destroy my people and mothers shall weep for their sons and women shall curse their wombs that bring forth fodder for the Beast to feed on.

Witness. Witness here that I shall lay him low.

DIAMOND *is close to* TOM *and makes a lunge.* RUBY *seeing what is happening grabs the gun from the table and points it at* DIAMOND. DIAMOND *stands with his arms out towards her.*

Ruby.

RUBY. I tell you already, I leavin' here tonight and you ain't go destroy dis child like you destroy everything in your life. I go kill you before you do that.

DIAMOND *holds out his hands and drops the knife.*

DIAMOND (*walks towards* RUBY). Ruby, yuh wrong. Don't believe dem. They lie. We strong. We strong. We strong enough we could save each other.

RUBY. You ain't making me crazy like you. Speechifying like you some Midnight Robber.

DIAMOND. Turn away de gun, Ruby. Don't be what dey want to make yuh. They lie.

DIAMOND *tries to take hold of the gun from* RUBY. *She wrestles with him and the gun goes off.* PEARL, RUBY *and* DIAMOND *cry out.* DIAMOND *takes hold of* RUBY*'s face.*

We are what we dream. Nobody can make you into what you are not. We are blessed if we believe we are. This world is ours.

SELDOM *appears at the door. He sees* RUBY *holding the gun.* PEARL *takes up the sculpture weakly and sits on a chair clutching it to her.*

SELDOM. Ruby, Miss Pearl. Dey hear shot fire from inside here. What happen? Police go have to come now for sure /

PEARL. Seldom, nothing ain't happen. You seeing all ah we here in front yuh face. Right? Right, so everyting good.

TOM. Well, officer. Everything is in order here, so you won't mind if I go. I have a US vessel awaiting my return.

RUBY (*points the gun at him*). Well, you ain't leavin' me. A pregnant bride-to-be can be a handy passport. For all sort ah ting. You going to need me to get past that crowd screaming outside. They done hear gunshot. And everybody know this house, Alma. If I scream now you ain't going nowhere. Believe me. But I can get us past. And Seldom go take we in his car. Right, Seldom? Take we both out ah here.

TOM (*thinks quickly*). Ha. Trumped again, my treasure.

He hold out his hand for the gun. RUBY *stows the gun away in her clothing.*

In that case we must bid you all farewell. Beat the path, my fair lady.

TOM *takes the valise from* RUBY. RUBY *walks over to* PEARL *and stands in front of her.*

Beat.

PEARL *grabs hold of* RUBY*'s hand and pulls her down towards her.* PEARL *grips her face.*

PEARL (*whispers- and it doesn't matter if we hear it*). I forgive you.

She kisses RUBY*'s mouth firmly.*

RUBY *stands back confused. She heads towards the front door where* TOM *is waiting, turns and looks back at* DIAMOND. *She seems to think about taking a step towards him but then turns back and exits followed by* TOM.

SELDOM *stands in the room not sure what to do.*

Seldom.

SELDOM. Miss Pearl?

PEARL. So tell me true. Dem mafia man and dem American road people, is really just de money dey want or is my son blood dey want in truth?

SELDOM. Well, Miss Pearl, dat is a hard one. I ain't go lie to yuh. Yuh see de deal was police wasn't go reach in here till de mafia man and dem had come and get dey money and do whatever else it is dey go do. But now since gun shoot off and people hear it quite in de road, dey callin' for police. You hearin' dem. Dem fellas ain't really go want to be here now. So, me ain't know nuh.

PEARL. So, if dese people get dey money dey go leave my son alone?

SELDOM. I suppose dat go make sense all round. It too messy for the Yanks dem now. Dey probably just take dey money and gone.

PEARL. Den Seldom, help me out here. Diamond, look in dat case over there under where de statue was.

DIAMOND *moves over to where* PEARL *is indicating and opens the plinth.*

Take out de box what in dere. Now hand dat to Seldom please. Now Seldom, I askin' you to take dis box and give it to those people. Tell all ah dem dat is de money dat dey want for my son. Dey doh need to come inside my house. If dey get dat dey could just left we alone. Seldom, I know you since you is a child, runnin' wild on de road and dis one time I trustin' you to do what I ask yuh. Y'hear? I know you go do good for me.

SELDOM. Alright, Miss Pearl. Yes. Hear de ting. I go tell de officers dem, I check out de scene here for meself and everything good and secure. No need to investigate.

PEARL. God bless yuh. Goodnight.

SELDOM. Goodnight den. I gone.

SELDOM *leaves.* DIAMOND *turns towards his mother.*

PEARL. My whole life I spend making money for dat man. I break meh back, meh foot, meh heart, everyting, working for he. I had was to be stupid if I wasn't going to make sure and take for meself what he owe meh. If I ain't watch out for me, I know it ain't have nobody else go do it. You see people like us, son, we understand it ain't some lifestyle but just life it-damn-self dat we must fight for. We know what it is to 'eat de bread de devil knead'. And, sorry child, dat legacy pass down to you from me and right back down de line. But if I sell meh soul den it must buy your freedom and it go break dat damn chain.

DIAMOND *goes on his knees in front of* PEARL.

I didn't understand dat de first time. Then, me just give yuh birth but dis time I want to give yuh life.

PEARL *holds the statue to him.*

You is my child and you was right. De birthright belong to you. But dis is it here. I givin' it to you. You feel you never had a mother, you ain't got legacy? Hold dis and you go always know dey can't ever take it just so.

Taking hold of the statue DIAMOND *finds it is covered with* PEARL*'s blood.*

DIAMOND. What…

PEARL (*life is fading from her*). Doh mind dat. Is not you what do dis, son. You understand dat? I need you to believe dat. But listen. I leave you once before and you come back to me. And now we know dat I can't never leave you. De whole time I was dere wid you. Take dis and when yuh watch it you go know all dat I am, all dat make me, go always be there inside you. De legacy pass down through de blood. It don't lost, it still here. No crossing of sea or land could take it away. You always had a mother, child, and she always love yuh. You hear me. So, doh cry, beloved man. We are what we know ourselves to be.

With their foreheads touching, right, left then centre (according to Orisha) She sings faintly.

'Safasa Mama,
Maliweh, Saki batni Mama...'

PEARL *stops.* DIAMOND *touches her face and she doesn't move.*

DIAMOND *kisses her mouth and looks into her eyes before closing them shut.*

He kneels back and holds onto the statue. He looks at the blood on PEARL*'s dress.*

DIAMOND *rests his head on* PEARL*'s lap and closes his eyes. The lights go out.*

The End.

www.nickhernbooks.co.uk

@nickhernbooks